BAKU
TRAVEL GUIDE
2023

RANDY S. LESNAR

Baku Travel Guide 2023

Discovering The Amazing City of Baku: Unveiling Hidden Gems, Cultural Wonders, Historical Landmarks for First-Timers

BY

RANDY S. LESNAR

Table Of Content

Good Morning Baku

My Holiday

A Synopsis of Baku History

Population in Baku

Culture

Climate in Baku

Religious Practices

What makes Baku a Popular Tourist Destination

Chapter 1: Travel Preparation

Best Time to Visit

How to Get There

Currency

Language

Internet and Calling

Chapter 2: Entry Requirements

Why Entry Requirements

Entry Requirements for a Visa to Baku

Who must Obtain a Visa to Visit Baku?

Visa Categories

Visa Application Process

Evidence of Sufficient Funding

Vaccinations

Chapter 3: Accommodation and Price Options

Hotels and Resort on a Budget

Luxury Hotels and Resorts

Vacation Rentals and Apartments

Campouts and Glamping

Chapter 4: Acceptable Étiquettes and NightLife

Dress Tips for Men

Dress Tips for Women

Food

Drinks

Street Food and Snacks

Best Eateries and Coffee Shops

Dining Manners

Chapter 5: Transportation Options and Costs in Baku

Buses

Subway

Trams

Taxis

Ride-Hailing Services

Car Rentals

Walking and Bicycle

Bike-Sharing Schemes

Train

Chapter 6: Essential tips you must know as a first Timer

Bring Some Cash with You

Where to Find an Exchanger

Consider Travel Insurance

Medical Care Services

Health Tips for Travelers

LQBTQ+Acceptance

Emergency Contacts

Laws

Chapter 7: Planning and Financial Management

The Need for Managing Finances when Traveling

Savings Tips for Travelers

Tips for Bargaining and Negotiating

Tax-Free Shopping and Refund

Top Markets

Chapter 8: Tourist Attractions and Fun Activities

Tourist Attractions

Educational Attractions and Museums

Festivals and Events

Enjoyable sports and activities

Chapter 9: Day Trips and Excursions

Explore Wildlife and Nature

Overview of a Solo Trip

Is a Solo Trip Safe?

Websites, Applications, and Resources that are Useful

Conclusion

Good Morning Baku

Welcome to Baku, the capital and biggest city of Azerbaijan, a dynamic city! Baku, which is tucked away on the Caspian Sea's coast, is a remarkable synthesis of historic tradition and contemporary design. This vibrant city provides a unique travel experience with its rich history, diversified culture, and lively vitality.

Baku is a city where the past and current coexist in perfect harmony. The Old City, also known as Icherisheher, is the city's historical center and a repository of historical and architectural marvels. It is a UNESCO World Heritage site. You will come across historic mosques, caravanserais, and palaces as you meander through the city's winding cobblestone alleyways. Each of these structures tells an enthralling tale of the city's history.

The majestic Maiden Tower is among Baku's most recognizable sights. This mysterious cylindrical building, which towers over the city's skyline and has been standing for more than 800 years, is still steeped in mystery and lore. For stunning views of the city and the Caspian Sea, go to the summit.

The Flame Towers are a further architectural wonder that exemplifies Baku's contemporary aspect. The cityscape is dominated by these three gleaming towers, which are lit at night to create a spellbinding scene. They stand in for the abundant oil and gas resources of the nation and are a representation of Azerbaijan's rising importance in the global energy market.

Baku has a vibrant cultural scene in addition to its architectural wonders. Explore the city's many museums and galleries, including the Azerbaijan National Museum of History, which has a sizable collection of objects dating back thousands of years. The Heydar Aliyev Center, with its futuristic architecture and exhibits presenting modern art and cultural heritage, is a must-see for art fans.

The gastronomic delicacies of Baku will thrill food enthusiasts. Russian, Turkish, and Persian cuisines have all affected the city's diversified gastronomic scene. Enjoy tasty pilaf, fragrant kebabs, and a variety of traditional Azerbaijani sweets. A unique culinary delicacy, the regional specialty of plov is a rice dish cooked with saffron, pork, and dried fruits.

Baku is close to beautiful natural settings for outdoor lovers. The Absheron Peninsula is renowned for its beautiful coastline, where visitors may relax on sand-filled beaches or explore the area's unusual mud volcanoes. With its historic rock sculptures and breathtaking natural formations, Gobustan National Park, a UNESCO World Heritage site, is a paradise for outdoor lovers.

Baku's thriving nightlife comes to life as dusk strikes. Trendy pubs, rooftop lounges, and nightclubs where you can dance the night away are all around the city. The city's major thoroughfare, Nizami Street, is transformed into a busy pedestrian promenade that offers a vibrant ambiance full of opportunities for eating, shopping, and entertainment.

Baku has much to offer everyone, regardless of your interests in history, architecture, or culture, or just want a great vacation experience. This vibrant city will make a lasting impression on your travel with its intriguing combination of old history and contemporary vitality. Prepare yourself to get engrossed in Baku's enchantment and learn the secrets that make this city a magical destination unlike any other.

My Holiday

At Heydar Aliyev International Airport in Baku, Azerbaijan, I could feel the excitement growing within me as I got off the aircraft. I was eager to delve into this lovely city's rich history, lively culture, and gorgeous views as I started my long-awaited holiday.

I traveled to the hotel, which was in the center of the city and had breathtaking views of the Caspian Sea. I was instantly drawn to the cityscape's mix of contemporary construction and classic features. It was as if the past and the future were flawlessly woven together in Baku.

I decided to tour Icherisheher, or the Old City of Baku, on my first day there. This UNESCO World Heritage Site's twisting, winding lanes were adorned with gorgeous mosques, attractive gardens, and old stone walls. The feeling of traveling back in time and the ambiance from the Middle Ages had me spellbound.

I couldn't resist going to the famous Maiden Tower, a tall building that has come to represent Baku. As I made my way to the summit, I gasped at the panoramic views of the city, with its contemporary skyline standing out against its historic surroundings. It was the ideal location for some priceless pictures.

The Flame Towers, a trio of skyscrapers that dominate Baku's skyline, were one of the highlights of my vacation. As dusk fell, the towers lit up in a spectacular light display that bathed the city in vibrant hues and patterns. It was a spellbinding sight that made me marvel at Baku's progress and creativity.

I went to the Heydar Aliyev Center, a late Zaha Hadid architectural masterpiece, to learn more about Azerbaijan's rich cultural legacy. The building's flowing contours and eye-catching white front were stunning to see. I found a treasure trove of historical, artistic, and interactive displays that highlighted the nation's customs and accomplishments.

A trip to Baku would not be complete without sampling some of its gastronomic treats. I ate enough of regional cuisine, including plov (rice pilaf), dolma (stuffed grape leaves), and mouthwatering kebabs. I enjoyed every morsel because the tastes were so wonderful. I also perused the crowded Taza Bazaar, where I discovered a wide selection of fresh foods, spices, and regional delights to bring back as gifts.

I took the chance to go outside of Baku and see the natural beauty of the neighboring areas in between my investigations of the city. I set out on a day excursion to the Gobustan National Park, which is well-known for its historic rock carvings and mud volcanoes. I was taken to another time and place by the fantastical landscapes and old tales carved into the rocks.

On a different day, I went to the charming village of Quba, which is tucked away in the Caucasus Mountains' foothills. The stunning vistas of the snow-capped peaks and green valleys throughout the beautiful drive were amazing. I spent my time in Quba immersing myself in the community's culture by discovering local crafts, seeing ancient mosques, and tasting delectable honey.

I couldn't help but feel grateful for the great experiences I had when my trip to Baku came to a close. I will never forget the city's distinctive fusion of history, culture, and natural beauty. Baku had exceeded all of my expectations, and I knew I would treasure these experiences for a lifetime.

A Synopsis of Baku History

The history of Baku, the capital of Azerbaijan, is lengthy and diversified, spanning many millennia. Baku, which is located on the western shore of the Caspian Sea, has long been a significant hub for regional commerce, culture, and politics. Here is a synopsis of Baku's past:

Medieval and Prehistoric Periods:
The Baku region has been inhabited by humans since the Stone Age, according to the oldest evidence. Throughout its history, the area has been inhabited by a variety of peoples, including the Scythians, Medes, Persians, and Romans. The Sassanian Empire took control of the city in the fifth century AD.

The Islamic Era:
Baku developed to become a significant Muslim stronghold and a hub of Islamic culture with the arrival of Islam in the 7th century. The Shirvanshahs, a native dynasty that founded the Shirvanshahs State in the 9th

century, took control of the city after the Arabs had conquered it in the eighth century.

Turkic and Mongol Invasions:
The Mongols, headed by Genghis Khan and subsequently by his grandson Hulagu Khan, attacked Baku in the 13th century. The Seljuks and the Khwarazmians were among the Turkic invaders that came after the Mongol era. Baku saw considerable devastation and depopulation during this time.

Persian Rule and the Safavids:
Baku was ruled by the Safavid dynasty of Persia in the 16th century. The Safavids rebuilt the city's defenses and expanded Baku as a significant port and commerce hub. During this time, the city flourished and drew traders from Europe, Central Asia, and India.

Russian Infiltration:
Baku was influenced by the Russian Empire at the beginning of the 19th century. The Russians understood the city's strategic and economic significance, notably its

enormous oil reserves. Baku became one of the world's top oil-producing locations as a result of the growth of the oil industry in the late 19th and early 20th centuries.

Sputnik Era:

Baku joined the Azerbaijan Democratic Republic and then the Azerbaijan Soviet Socialist Republic in the Soviet Union after the 1917 Russian Revolution. Rapid industrialization, modernization, and the growth of the oil sector occurred in the city.

Independence in Today's World:

After the Soviet Union fell apart in 1991, Azerbaijan achieved its independence, and Baku was designated as the nation's capital. With the growth of contemporary infrastructure, the erection of skyscrapers, and the revitalization of its cultural legacy, the city has experienced tremendous transition and development.

Baku is now a thriving, multicultural metropolis that harmoniously combines its historic origins with contemporary influences. In addition to hosting the first

European Games in 2015 and the Eurovision Song Contest in 2012, it is a significant center for commerce, tourism, and international events. Visitors from all over the globe are drawn to Baku by its extensive architectural history, which includes the medieval Old City (Icherisheher), the Palace of the Shirvanshahs, and the contemporary Flame Towers. The city is still a significant hub for the oil and gas sector, as well as a focus for the arts and culture in the area.

Population in Baku

Approximately 2.3 million individuals called Baku home. Please take notice that migration, natural growth, or other reasons might have caused the population estimates to vary since then.

Due to its advantageous position on the western shore of the Caspian Sea, Baku has benefited greatly from the growth of its culture, economy, and history. The city has 12 administrative districts and covers an area of around 2,200 square kilometers (850 square miles).

Baku's population is varied and cosmopolitan, reflecting the city's past and its status as a significant economic and cultural hub in the area. Azerbaijanis, the biggest ethnic group in the nation, make up the majority of the population. But many other ethnic groups, including Russians, Armenians, Talysh, Lezgins, Jews, and others, also call Baku home. The colorful and cosmopolitan vibe of the city is a result of the city's rich blend of cultures.

Baku's population has increased significantly over the years as a result of urbanization, industrialization, and employment prospects. People from rural areas and other parts of the nation come to the city, which serves as Azerbaijan's main economic center, in quest of better prospects and a higher quality of life.

Baku has a very youthful population, with a significant part of the population under the age of 35. The city's cultural scene, nightlife, and general way of life are all influenced by this young population, which also gives the city a lively vibe.

Baku has recently experienced substantial urban expansion and renovation initiatives, which have included the creation of new residential neighborhoods, business buildings, and infrastructural upgrades. These programs are intended to accommodate the expanding population and improve the livability of the city.

It is important to note that Baku has seen considerable emigration, notably among young professionals looking for chances to study or jobs overseas. Many nations have struggled with brain drain, as it is popularly known, and Azerbaijan is no exception. However, the city still draws a sizable number of foreigners who come to work, study, or conduct different commercial ventures.

The people of Baku are diverse, young, and have a blend of traditional and contemporary influences. The city is a significant hub of Azerbaijan's social, political, and economic life due to its advantageous position, economic prospects, and cultural attractions.

Culture

Baku has a vibrant and varied culture that is shaped by the city's history, geography, and many ethnic communities that call it home. Baku's cultural landscape is a harmonic synthesis of historic Azerbaijani components with contemporary Western and regional influences. Here is a thorough explanation of Baku culture:

Baku is well-steeped in Azerbaijani traditions, which are reflected in its cultural customs, art, music, and food. The community values Azerbaijan's rich cultural legacy, which includes traditional poetry storytelling, and ethnic dances like Yalli and Meykhana. Baku continues to perform and appreciate traditional musical instruments like the tar (long-necked lute) and kamancha (spike violin).

Baku's architecture is a reflection of the city's history and the several civilizations that had dominated the area. The Old City (Icheri Sheher) is a distinctive fusion of medieval, Islamic, and European architectural forms and is a UNESCO World Heritage site. The renowned Flame Towers and contemporary buildings dotting the city skyline highlight Baku's architectural modernity.

Multiculturalism: Azerbaijanis, Russians, Armenians, Tatars, Jews, and Lezgins are just a few of the ethnic groups that call Baku home. An inclusive and diversified society has benefited from this multicultural atmosphere. Through festivals, exhibits, and events that highlight various ethnic customs, costumes, and cuisines, Baku celebrates cultural diversity.

Baku is renowned for its thriving cultural scene, which includes a wide variety of museums and cultural organizations. A few examples of the city's diverse cultural offerings are the Heydar Aliyev Center, the Museum of Modern Art, the Azerbaijan National Museum of History, and the Azerbaijan Carpet Museum. These organizations preserve and advance Azerbaijani history, art, and culture while giving national and international artists a stage on which to exhibit their creations.

Poetry and literature: Baku has a rich literary history, with notable Azerbaijani authors and poets making important contributions to the field of literature. The city holds many literary festivals and activities that together authors, poets, and readers. In Baku, the tradition of great poets like Nizami Ganjavi and Mirza Alakbar Sabir is treasured and honored.

Baku is a sanctuary for food enthusiasts, and Azerbaijani cuisine is varied and savory. The city provides a large selection of traditional foods, including kebabs, pilaf, dolma (stuffed grape leaves), and several soups and stews. Azerbaijani, Middle Eastern, Mediterranean, and European cuisines are combined in Baku's eateries to appeal to a variety of preferences.

Festivals & festivities: Baku has some festivals and festivities all year long to highlight the cultural richness of the city. The International Mugham Festival, the

Novruz Bayram (Persian New Year), and the Gurban Bayram (Eid al-Adha) are a few of the important cultural occasions that emphasize traditional music, dance, and art forms. These celebrations bring together residents and visitors to showcase the diversity of Azerbaijani culture.

Recreation and Sports: Baku has become a major venue for international athletic events. The European Games, UEFA Europa League Final, and Formula 1 Azerbaijan Grand Prix have all been held in the city. Baku's culture is heavily influenced by sports, and there are easily accessible facilities for basketball, volleyball, football, and aquatic sports.

Climate in Baku

The city of Baku, which is bordered by the Caspian Sea, has a semiarid climate with four distinct seasons. Baku's climate is impacted by both the sea and the adjacent mountains, which results in unusual weather patterns all year long.

June to August

Baku has hot, dry summers with typical daily highs of 25°C to 35°C (77°F to 95°F). However, sporadic heat waves can raise temperatures exceeding 40°C (104°F). During this time of year, the city has very little rain and humidity, which offers some respite from the heat. The air from the Caspian Sea helps keep coastal regions' temperatures in check.

September to November

The weather is usually moderate and pleasant in Baku during the autumn. From 15°C to 25°C (59°F to 77°F) in September to 5°C to 15°C (41°F to 59°F) in November, temperatures steadily decrease. During this time, there is a modest amount of rain in the city, with October being the wettest. As the leaves change color, the surroundings take on stunning hues of orange and gold.

December to February

Baku has comparatively moderate winters when compared to other regions of the nation. The daily average temperature is between 3°C and 8°C (37°F and 46°F), while the overnight low is usually around 0°C (32°F). Although it does not snow often and is typically light, snow showers might happen sometimes. It's the coldest in January. Strong gusts may make it seem colder even if the city has rather dry weather throughout the winter.

March to May

Baku's spring is a transitional season marked by swiftly shifting weather patterns. From 8°C to 15°C (46°F to 59°F) in March to 15°C to 25°C (59°F to 77°F) in May, temperatures climb steadily. The wettest month in the city is April, which also gets considerable rainfall. An aesthetically pleasing season, spring provides blossoming flowers and lush vegetation.

The Caspian Sea, which works as a moderating effect, and the close-by mountains, which operate as a barrier for certain weather systems, have an impact on Baku's climate. Around 200–300 mm (8–12 inches) of precipitation falls on the city each year, with the majority of this falling between the months of autumn and spring. Baku is a well-liked vacation destination for travelers seeking a variety of weather conditions throughout the year because of its geographic position and temperature.

Religious Practices

Islam is the most popular religion in Baku and Azerbaijan as a whole. The city is a center of religious variety due to the presence of several other religious groups there as well.

Islam:

In Baku, Islam is the religion that is most extensively practiced, with the majority of the people identifying as Muslims. Baku highlights the fact that Azerbaijan is a primarily Shia Muslim nation. The majority of people are Shia Muslims, although there is also a small Sunni Muslim minority.

Mosques:

Numerous mosques can be found all across Baku, acting as Muslim communities' spiritual and cultural hubs. The Bibi-Heybat Mosque, a wonderful architectural wonder outside of Baku, is one of the most notable mosques in the area. Shia Muslims place a tremendous deal of value on this mosque, which draws both domestic and foreign tourists. Another well-known mosque where Muslims congregate for prayers and religious occasions is the Taza Pir Mosque, which is situated in the center of the city.

Spiritual Habits:

The Muslim community in Baku adheres to Islamic customs and traditions. Jumu'ah, or Friday communal prayers, are a significant component of the weekly religious schedule. Muslims keep a strict fast from dawn to sunset throughout the holy month of Ramadan, as well as extra prayers and charitable deeds. The holidays of Eid al-Fitr and Eid al-Adha, which commemorate the conclusion of Ramadan, and Prophet Abraham's willingness to sacrifice his son, respectively, are observed with tremendous fervor.

Tolerance of Religion:

There has always been religious cooperation and tolerance in Baku. The whole nation of Azerbaijan takes pleasure in having a secular governmental system where religion and politics are kept apart. This strategy has helped to create a climate where different religious groups may live in harmony and exercise their beliefs.

Additional Religious Groups:

Baku is home to several different religious groups in addition to Islam, including:

Christianity: Baku's little Christian population is served by Christian churches. An important venue of worship for the Orthodox Christian population is the Russian Orthodox Church, which is situated close to the city center.

Judaism: There is a tiny Jewish population in Baku and synagogues that are used for prayer and community events can be found there. Baku is home to a sizable community of Mountain Jews, who have a unique cultural and religious background.

Other Religions: Because Baku is a cosmopolitan city, there are also adherents of other faiths there, including the Bahá' Faith, Buddhism, and Hinduism, among others.

Despite being somewhat modest, these communities help the city's religious variety.

Interreligious Conversation and Cultural Exchange:
Baku actively encourages interfaith conversation and cultural interaction to build peace and understanding across various religious groups. To promote peace, tolerance, and respect among people of different religious origins, the city sponsors conferences, seminars, and other activities.

Baku is a city where the majority of the people identify as Muslims and Islam is the main religion. With Christian, Jewish, and other religious populations present, the city does, however, encourage religious pluralism. Baku's religious environment is a reflection of its long history of religious tolerance and harmonious cohabitation, which has helped to make it a thriving center for interfaith discussion and cross-cultural interaction.

What makes Baku a Popular Tourist Destination

In recent years, Baku has quickly become a well-liked tourism destination. Baku provides visitors with a distinctive and unforgettable experience because of its fascinating history, beautiful architecture, active culture, and spectacular natural beauty. Listed below is a thorough explanation of why Baku has grown to be a popular travel destination:

Baku has a wonderful history that goes back thousands of years. It also has beautiful architecture. The Old City, also known as Icherisheher, is located in the city and is a walled medieval complex with historic sites and structures that is on the UNESCO World Heritage List. The Shirvanshah Palace, the Maiden Tower, and some mosques, caravanserais, and hammams that highlight the city's architectural history may all be found in the Old City.

Modern Skyline & Futuristic Structures: Baku has recently seen substantial growth, leaving it with a breathtaking modern skyline that contrasts with its historic origins. With structures like the Flame Towers, Heydar Aliyev Center, and Crystal Hall as monuments, the city is well known for its avant-garde and inventive architecture. These recognizable buildings serve as symbols of Baku's change and draw visitors from all over the globe.

Cultural Diversity and a Thriving Arts Scene: Baku is a crossroads of civilizations, fusing elements of the East and the West. The museums, art galleries, and theaters in the city all showcase its rich cultural legacy. The National Museum of History, Museum of Modern Art, and Azerbaijan Carpet Museum are only a few examples of cultural establishments that display the nation's creative history and modern inventiveness. The city's cultural environment is further enriched by the various international festivals and events that Baku organizes, including the Baku Jazz Festival and the Baku International Film Festival.

Beautiful Seaside Location: Baku, which is located on the Caspian Sea's coast, provides gorgeous waterfront views and a relaxing seaside atmosphere. The Baku Boulevard, the city's lovely coastal promenade, spans many kilometers and is the ideal location for strolls, bike rides, and other outdoor sports. The Boulevard is a well-liked meeting place for both residents and visitors since it is bordered by parks, cafés, restaurants, and entertainment establishments.

Baku is the ideal location to indulge in Azerbaijani cuisine, which is a delicious blend of tastes from the Middle East, Central Asia, and the Mediterranean. Traditional tea rooms, quaint eateries, and food stands selling a range of delectable foods including plov (pilaf), kebabs, dolma (stuffed grape leaves), and baklava can be found all around the city. The cuisine scene in Baku also has foreign eateries that appeal to a variety of tastes and preferences.

Outdoor Adventures & Natural Beauty: Outside the city boundaries, Baku is home to breathtaking natural scenery. Visitors may visit the Absheron Peninsula, which is just a short drive away, and is home to unusual mud volcanoes, the recognizable Yanar Dag (Burning Mountain), and the historic fire temple of Ateshgah. Prehistoric rock sculptures are on display at the Gobustan National Park, a UNESCO World Heritage Site, which also provides chances for trekking and environmental exploration.

Warm Hospitality and Safety: Baku is renowned for its kind residents who welcome tourists with open arms. The city has a good reputation for safety, which attracts travelers looking for a safe and fun experience.

Baku's allure as a travel destination is derived from its fascinating fusion of ancient history and contemporary development, cultural variety, spectacular architecture, natural beauty, and friendly people.

Chapter 1: Travel Preparation

Make a thorough packing list before traveling to Baku, the capital of Azerbaijan, to make sure you have everything you need for a relaxing and pleasurable stay. The following is a thorough explanation of how to prepare for your trip to Baku and what to pack:

Clothing:

Pack lightweight, loose-fitting clothing made of breathable materials, such as cotton or linen, since Baku has scorching summers.

Dress modestly: Given that Azerbaijan is primarily a Muslim nation, it is advised to do so, particularly while visiting places of worship. Dress in clothing that covers your knees and shoulders.

Bring comfortable shoes that are appropriate for visiting the city's streets and sights since Baku is a walkable city.

Pack a sweater or light jacket for layering since evenings may become chilly, especially in the spring and fall.

Travel papers:

Make sure your passport is valid for at least six months after the day you want to travel.

Visa: Verify your country's criteria for a visa and apply if one is required.

Carry printed copies of your trip documents as a backup, including your passport, visa, travel insurance, and hotel bookings.

Electronics:

Bring a universal power adapter to charge your electronics since Azerbaijan utilizes Type C and Type F power outlets.

Bring your cell phone and charger to stay connected, and don't forget to pack a charger.

Camera: Use a camera or a dependable smartphone with a decent camera to capture Baku's stunning vistas.

Health and Medication:

Prescription drugs: If you need to pack enough of any prescription drugs for the length of your vacation, do so.

Include bandages, painkillers, antihistamines, and any other personal prescriptions in a basic first-aid pack.

It is advised to get travel insurance that includes coverage for medical emergencies, trip cancellation, and lost or stolen possessions.

Banking and Finance:

Local money: The Azerbaijani Manat (AZN) is used as money in that country. Bring some local money with you or make withdrawals when you are there.

Carry credit or debit cards that are accepted worldwide for ease. To prevent any problems using your card overseas, let your bank know about your vacation intentions.

Additional Items:

Maps and travel guides help navigate cities and learn about their attractions. You can also download travel apps.

Consider using language translation software to communicate with people in your area who may not speak English.

Bring travel locks to protect your belongings and hotel room.

It's important to note that Baku is a contemporary city with plenty of conveniences, so if necessary, you can quickly get any missed products locally. Keep in mind to prepare for the weather expected during your journey dates and the particular activities you want to participate in.

Best Time to Visit

Your tastes and the activities you want to do will have a big impact on when is the ideal time to visit Baku. Here is a thorough explanation of the various seasons and things to think about while making travel plans to Baku:

Spring - March to May:

A beautiful time to go to Baku is in the spring when the weather is moderate and the flowers are in bloom. The optimal range of temperatures for enjoying the city's parks and outdoor attractions is between 10°C (50°F) and 20°C (68°F). This time of year is especially pleasant for strolling along the renowned Baku Boulevard that runs beside the Caspian Sea.

Summertime - June to August

Baku has hot, dry summers with typical highs of 35°C (95°F) and lows of 25°C (77°F). The city has long, sunny days that are ideal for sightseeing and other outdoor activities. It's vital to remember that the high temperatures may sometimes be harsh, so it's crucial to drink enough water and seek cover when required.

Fall - September to November

Another great time to go to Baku is in the fall. Between 15°C (59°F) and 25°C (77°F), the temperatures start to drop. The parks and gardens of the city have lovely fall foliage, which makes the area charming. Additionally, the Formula 1 Azerbaijan Grand Prix, which draws spectators from all over the globe to Baku, takes place in September.

Winter - December to February

Temperatures in Baku during the winter range from 0°C (32°F) to 10°C (50°F), making them pleasant and reasonably cool. Even though it doesn't snow much, there are sometimes severe cold spells. This time of year might be a great time to travel if you appreciate wintertime activities like ice skating or interior destinations like museums and historical buildings. A variety of festive activities and entertainment are also offered at Baku's Winter Festival, which takes place in December.

Other aspects to think about

Tourist Season: The summer months, especially July and August, are when Baku sees its busiest travel season due to the influx of foreign tourists. As a result, it's possible for crowds to form at famous locations, and hotel rates are often higher. Consider going in the shoulder seasons of spring or fall if you want a more sedate atmosphere.

Festivals & Events: Baku organizes a wide range of cultural and athletic events all year long. Finding out whether there are any festivals or events that specifically connect with your hobbies might give your trip a whole new dimension.

Ramadan: It's crucial to be aware of regional traditions and practices if you want to visit Baku during the Islamic holy month of Ramadan (dates change each year dependent on the lunar calendar). Due to Muslims' observed fasting, many eateries may have reduced operation hours or restricted menus during daytime hours.

The ideal time to visit Baku will depend on your choices for the weather, how crowded it will be, and the things you want to do. While summer offers longer days and more dynamic energy, spring and fall often provide good weather and fewer visitors. If you prefer indoor activities and cultural events, winter may be an excellent alternative. When planning the perfect trip to Baku, keep these things in mind.

How to Get There

The Caspian Sea coast is home to Baku, the capital of Azerbaijan. You have a variety of options for getting to Baku, including flying, taking the train, and driving. Here is a thorough explanation of each choice:

By Air:

Air travel is the quickest and most practical method of getting to Baku. Heydar Aliyev International Airport (GYD), which has good connections to significant cities all over the globe, serves Baku. Here are the flight details to get there:

International Flights: You may book a flight to Heydar Aliyev International Airport with any significant international airline if you're flying in from outside of Azerbaijan. Direct flights from several major cities, including London, Paris, Istanbul, Dubai, Moscow, and many more, are available to Baku.

Check for domestic flights if you currently reside in Azerbaijan and want to go to Baku from another city within the nation. Domestic flights are offered by Azerbaijan Airlines (AZAL) between Baku and several significant cities, including Ganja, Nakhchivan, Lankaran, and Gabala.

You have three options for getting around Baku after landing at Heydar Aliyev International Airport: a taxi, ridesharing, or the airport shuttle.

By Train:

The railway system allows you to get to Baku if you want to travel by train. However, keep in mind that there aren't many international trains that go to Baku, so you may need to combine trains with buses or taxis for some of the trips. Here's how to take a train to go to Baku:

International Trains: Baku has a limited number of international rail services that link it to nearby nations. Take the train from Moscow, Russia to Baku, for instance, which often requires a transfer to Astara,

Azerbaijan. Similar rail connections exist between Baku and Tbilisi, Georgia.

Domestic Trains: You can go to Baku from other significant cities in Azerbaijan if you're already there. Domestic train services are run by Azerbaijan Railways, the nation's railroad business. As an example, you may get to Baku by rail from Ganja, Nakhchivan, or Lankaran.

You may use a cab or the city's public transit system to go where you're going after arriving at Baku's main train station.

By Road:

Baku is easily accessible by vehicle or bus, depending on your preference for flexibility and if you love driving. Here is how to go by car to Baku:

International Bus: Several international bus routes link Baku to the nations around it. For instance, you may get to Baku by bus from Istanbul, Turkey. These buses often cross international borders and may need transfers or bus changes.

Domestic Bus: You may locate domestic bus services from other cities in Azerbaijan to Baku if you are already in the country. Buses are a well-liked form of transportation, with frequent lines connecting Baku with important cities like Ganja, Nakhchivan, Lankaran, and others.

You may use GPS navigation or follow road signs to get to your precise location inside Baku after arriving there by bus or automobile.

Before making travel plans to Baku, it is advised to check the most recent travel advisories, visa requirements, and transit schedules since it is vital to remember that travel rules and limitations might change.

Currency

The Azerbaijani manat (AZN) is the legal currency in Baku. Since 1992, when the manat replaced the Soviet ruble as the country's official currency, Azerbaijan has used the manat. It serves as the only form of legal money for all domestic transactions.

Qpik is smaller units that are subsequently split into manats. 100 quick are equal to one manat. Qpik coins aren't often utilized in daily transactions, but; instead, manat banknotes are used for the great majority of transactions.

Banknotes: Different denominations of Azerbaijani manat banknotes are available. The most widely used banknotes as per my knowledge expire in September 2021 are the 1, 5, 10, 20, 50, and 100 manat denominations. These banknotes may be readily distinguished from one another because of their distinctive patterns, hues, and sizes. Popular individuals from Azerbaijan's history, culture, and architecture are often shown on the banknotes.

Coins: The Azerbaijani manat has numerous coin denominations, albeit they are less often used. The 1, 3, 5, 10, 20, and 50 Qpik coins are among them. The national emblems, historical sites, and cultural themes included on the coins often represent the nation's rich history.

Exchange rates: The foreign exchange market controls the Azerbaijani manat's exchange rate, which varies in value concerning other world currencies. It's vital to remember that exchange rates might fluctuate every day or even all day long. Azerbaijani manat may be exchanged for foreign money at authorized exchange offices, banks, or ATMs in Baku.

Acceptance: Most businesses in Baku, including hotels, restaurants, supermarkets, and stores, accept the manat as a means of payment. Especially in tourist districts and premium restaurants, many companies also routinely take foreign credit and debit cards. It is a good idea to have some cash on hand for minor purchases or in case you come across businesses that only take cash.

Manat banknotes are easily accessible across Baku at banks, exchange offices, and ATMs. ATMs are widely dispersed and provide both locals and international tourists manat money. However, it is advised to examine rates and fees to guarantee fair conversion rates. Major shopping malls and hotels could also provide currency exchange services.

It is usually advised for tourists to get acquainted with the most recent exchange rates and to be wary of any possible fraud or unauthorized currency conversion services.

Language

Azeri, often known as Azerbaijani, is the nation's official language and is mainly spoken in Baku. The Oghuz branch of the Turkic language family includes Azerbaijani, which is a Turkic language. Although Azerbaijani is widely spoken, English is also understood and spoken to varied degrees, particularly among younger people and in tourist regions. The language of Baku is described in full below, along with certain terms and phrases that are helpful to visitors:

Alphabet of Azerbaijan:

The Azerbaijani Latin script, a modified form of the Latin alphabet, is used in Azerbaijani. The English language uses a phonetic alphabet with 32 letters, each of which stands for a distinct sound.

Greetings and Foundational Words:

Greetings: Salam

Leaving: Sa olun

Gratitude: Tşkkür edirm

Indeed: Bli

No, Xeyr.

Kindly say: Xahiş edirm

I'm sorry, Başlayn

I apologize: Üzr istyirm

Are you an English speaker?: Is English used in this sentence?

Transportation:

Terminal: Hava liman

Transit: Metro

Uber: Taksil

An Avtobus.

Dmir yolu, the train

Admission: Bilet

What is the price? Is Neçydir?

What metro station is the closest?: Yaxn Metro Station Haradr?

Dining:

Cafeteria: Restoran

Food: Menyu

Aqua: Su

java: kahve

Tea: Çay

Check/Bill: Hesab

I'd like to place an order for Sifariş etm k istyirm

Directions:

Where is that?: Haradadr?

Avenue: Küç

Mercator: Meydan

Right: Sol

Correct: Sa

Immediately: Düz get

Diagram: Xrit

Sightseeing:

Muzey, a museum

Saray Palace

Old Town: Qdim HR

The Park

Parish: Kils

Moorish: Mscid

Memorial: Abid

Shopping:

Store/shop: Maaza

Shop: Bazar

Geyim, Geyim

Footwear: Ayaqqab

Reminder: Reminder

What is the price? Is Neçydir?

It's crucial to remember that although knowing a few basic Azerbaijani words and phrases can improve your experience and interactions with the locals, even though these phrases might be useful. An approachable effort to communicate in the native tongue is often welcomed and may make getting about Baku easier.

Internet and Calling

A thriving city, Baku provides its citizens and tourists with a variety of internet and telephony options. Baku boasts a sophisticated telecommunications infrastructure that guarantees dependable connection and effective communication choices for both personal and business usage. Baku is a contemporary city with a fast-expanding technology industry.

Baku's Internet services:

The internet infrastructure in Baku is strong, and high-speed broadband connections are prevalent all around the city. Internet service providers (ISPs) provide a range of choices, such as DSL, cable, fiber-optic, and wireless connections, to meet a range of demands and financial constraints.

Digital Subscriber Line (DSL) and cable internet services are available from some ISPs to Baku citizens. These connections provide dependable speeds and work well for routine internet tasks like streaming and surfing.

Fiber-optic: Due to its unmatched speed and dependability, fiber-optic internet is becoming more and more common in Baku. In the city, some ISPs provide fiber-optic connections, enabling customers to take advantage of very high download and upload rates. For heavy internet users, online gaming, video conferencing, and streaming high-definition material, fiber-optic connections are the best option.

Wireless: Wireless internet access is widely available in Baku. Users of smartphones, tablets, and other mobile devices may remain connected with the help of mobile network providers' 4G and 5G mobile data services. Free Wi-Fi hotspots are widely available in Baku's cafés, eateries, and public areas, enabling travelers to surf the internet while on the move.

Services for Calling in Baku:
To facilitate both local and international communication, Baku offers a wide variety of calling services.

Telephones on a landline: In Baku, landline services are widely accessible and provide dependable voice connections both inside the city and to neighboring regions of Azerbaijan. Landline packages are available from a variety of service providers with various calling plans and prices.

Mobile phones: In Baku, mobile network carriers provide a wide range of plans and substantial coverage to meet a range of requirements. Users may utilize local and international calls, text messaging, and mobile data services with both prepaid and postpaid choices.

Audio over Internet Protocol (VoIP) services, which let users conduct audio and video conversations online, are becoming more and more popular in Baku. Many locals and tourists use services like Skype, WhatsApp, and Viber to make free or inexpensive calls to other VoIP users across the world.

Making international calls is easy in Baku because of the many alternatives available. The availability of international calling plans and tariffs from service providers allows locals and guests to stay in touch with friends, family, and business associates all around the globe. Additionally, calling cards may be bought, enabling customers to make inexpensive overseas calls.

All things considered, Baku provides a wide array of internet and telephony services, guaranteeing that locals and tourists have access to dependable connections and communication choices. Baku's telecommunications infrastructure satisfies the requirements of a contemporary, technologically advanced metropolis, whether it be for online surfing, making local or international calls, or remaining connected on mobile devices.

Chapter 2: Entry Requirements

Please be aware that travel policies and prerequisites are subject to change, therefore it's important to confirm the most recent information from reputable travel websites or official Azerbaijani institutions like the embassy or consulate.

Passport: A current passport is required for entry into Baku. Make sure your passport is valid for at least six months after the day you want to travel. Additionally, at least one blank page should be included for visa stamps.

Visa: Depending on your country of citizenship, you could need one to enter Azerbaijan. ASAN Visa, Azerbaijan's electronic visa system, enables qualified passengers to apply for their visas online before departing. By completing the application form and paying the necessary costs, you may submit an ASAN Visa application via the official website (evisa.gov.az). The visa is typically granted within three business days and is good for one entrance with a 30-day maximum stay.

However, certain nations including Azerbaijan have visa-exempt arrangements, enabling their nationals to travel or do business without obtaining a visa. Among them are the nations that make up the European Union, the United States, Canada, Australia, New Zealand, Japan, South Korea, and several other nations. Verify the current visa requirements for your nationality since the visa exemption period may change.

COVID-19 admission criteria: Additional admission criteria can be in place as a result of the current COVID-19 epidemic. The current scenario will determine how often these needs alter. The following were some of the typical COVID-19 admission criteria for traveling to Baku as of my knowledge cutoff date:

a. Negative COVID-19 Test: Travelers could be asked to provide a negative PCR test result obtained within a certain window of time before departure. It's important to confirm the most recent specifications since the timetable might change. Rapid antigen tests and other acceptable testing techniques could also be accepted in certain nations.

b. immunization: As a requirement for entrance, certain nations or airlines may demand evidence of COVID-19 immunization. Check the unique needs of your circumstance to see if there are any differences in the recommended vaccinations and immunization procedures.

c. Health Declarations: It may be necessary for travelers to fill out health declaration papers with details about their previous travel experiences and present health.

d. Vaccination status, test findings, and the country of departure all affect the quarantine requirements. Upon arrival, certain passengers could be subject to quarantine, while others might be excused if they satisfy certain requirements.

It is crucial to keep informed by reviewing the official recommendations from the Azerbaijani authorities or speaking with your local embassy or consulate since these COVID-19 regulations are subject to change.

Travelers may sometimes need an invitation letter from a host or sponsoring organization in Azerbaijan, particularly for trips that are business- or work-related. This condition usually applies more to long-term stays or certain types of visas.

Travel Insurance: Having travel insurance that covers medical costs, trip cancellation, and other unexpected situations during your time in Baku is advised, however, it is not required.

It is important to confirm the most recent Baku entry criteria by checking authoritative sources or getting in touch with the Azerbaijani embassy or consulate in your country.

Why Entry Requirements

To preserve visitor and resident safety, security, and efficiency in Baku, the capital city of Azerbaijan, entry restrictions are essential. These criteria, which include passports, visas, and other relevant paperwork, are crucial in controlling the flow of individuals entering and leaving the nation. The following justifies the significance of admission criteria in Baku:

National Security: Entry rules provide the government with the ability to keep an eye on and manage foreign visitors. With the use of these procedures, the government can evaluate the possible threats posed by anyone trying to enter the country illegally or in a criminal or terrorist capacity. Strict admission procedures may serve as a deterrent and safeguard the population and nation's infrastructure.

Public health: It's crucial to protect the public's health to have entry restrictions, especially during major health emergencies like pandemics. To stop the spread of contagious illnesses, governments may put policies in place like health examinations, immunization records, or quarantine guidelines. Baku can prevent the admission of people who would be a health danger to the local community by enforcing entry rules, lowering the risk of disease outbreaks, and safeguarding public health.

Entry criteria are a crucial component of efficient border management. They make it possible for authorities to effectively process visitors, resulting in a quick and orderly admission procedure. Baku can efficiently manage resources, simplify immigration operations, and keep order at ports of entry by defining clear entrance requirements. This promotes favorable impressions and supports the city's image as a welcoming destination by enabling a more seamless experience for both visitors and locals.

Entry criteria aid in regulating immigration and limiting demographic shifts. They make it possible for the government to control the number of people entering the nation, stop unlawful immigration, and guarantee adherence to immigration laws. The interests of both foreign residents and local labor are protected by these standards, which also aid in the enforcement of residence laws, work permit programs, and visa limits.

Entry criteria are important for efficient economic planning and growth. Authorities may assess tourist patterns, calculate visitor spending, and decide on infrastructure development, investment possibilities, and marketing tactics by gathering statistics on visitor arrivals. Accurate visitor demographic and behavior data may help tourist activities be tailored to certain target audiences, boosting the industry's total economic effect on Baku.

Bilateral Agreements and Reciprocity: Entry criteria are a way for nations to be in compliance with bilateral agreements and to be reciprocal with one another. Baku may establish reciprocal agreements with other countries and guarantee equitable treatment for its nationals going abroad by setting entrance limits and criteria. These agreements may boost collaboration in a variety of industries, including commerce, education, and tourism, as well as strengthen diplomatic ties and cultural exchanges.

It is crucial to remember that to prevent passengers from being confused or inconvenienced, admission procedures must be open, consistent, and adequately stated. Like many other cities throughout the globe, Baku understands the importance of entrance restrictions as a key element of public health, effective border administration, immigration control, economic planning, and international relations.

Entry Requirements for a Visa to Baku

Types of Visas

There are several different visas available in Azerbaijan, including transit, business, and tourist visas. Depending on the sort of visa you are seeking, there may be different special criteria.

Visa Waivers

Some nations and Azerbaijan have agreements that let their nationals enter without a visa or get one upon arrival. Travelers without a visa may have restrictions on their stay time and intended use of their visit. It is crucial to confirm if your nation qualifies for visa exemption.

Visa Request

You must typically submit an application to the Azerbaijani Embassy or Consulate in your home country, or via a designated visa application facility, to get a Baku visa. Depending on the accessibility of such services, the application may be filed in person or online.

Required Paperwork

Although the particular paperwork needed for a Baku visa may differ, generally speaking, you will need the following:

a. Passport must be current for at least six months beyond the expected length of stay in Azerbaijan. At least one blank page must be included for the visa stamp.

b. Visa Application Form: The visa application form must be correctly completed and signed. While some nations may offer an online application process, others can need a paper application.

c. You will need current passport-sized photos that adhere to the required specifications for size, background color, and appearance.

d. Proof of Accommodation: You can be asked to provide documentation proving your lodging arrangements while visiting Baku, such as hotel bookings or a letter of invitation from a host.

e. Proof of Sufficient Funds: You may need to provide evidence that you have the money to meet your costs while traveling to Azerbaijan. This might be a letter of sponsorship, a bank statement, or traveler's checks.

f. Travel Schedule: It is often necessary to provide a thorough schedule of your intended activities while visiting Azerbaijan, including confirmed flight information.

g. Letter of Invitation: If you are visiting Azerbaijan for business, you may require a letter of invitation from the host firm or organization.

h. Travel insurance: Having travel insurance that pays for medical costs, repatriation, and emergency evacuation is advised if you want to visit Azerbaijan.

i. Visa charge: The process of applying for a visa often entails a non-refundable charge. Depending on the kind and length of the visa, the fee may change.

Additional Conditions

Your employer's No Objection Certificate (NOC), a certificate of employment, or a clearing of your criminal history may be requested in certain circumstances as extra supporting documentation.

Processing Period

Depending on the embassy or consulate you apply to, as well as the kind of visa you are seeking, the processing period for a Baku visa might vary. To account for processing delays, it is suggested to submit your application well in advance of the day you expect to travel.

Keep in mind that these details are based on my understanding as of September 2021 and that visa regulations are subject to change. For the most recent and correct information on Baku visa requirements, it is crucial to visit the official website of the Azerbaijani Embassy or Consulate or to speak with the appropriate authorities.

Who must Obtain a Visa to Visit Baku?

Visa-free regime: Citizens of many nations are now able to enter Azerbaijan without a visa. The Commonwealth of Independent States (CIS) members, Turkey, Iran, Georgia, Belarus, Moldova, Ukraine, Uzbekistan, and a few more are among these nations. Depending on the nationality, different lengths of stay may be permitted under the visa-free entrance.

Electronic Visa (e-Visa): People from a lot of nations who aren't entitled to admission without a visa may get an electronic visa to go to Azerbaijan. With the e-Visa, you may apply for a visa online quickly and easily without having to go to an embassy or consulate. Before their travels, it enables passengers to get their visas online. The 30-day stay is permitted with the e-Visa, which is good for a single entrance.

Visa-on-arrival: At the international airports in Baku, certain nationals of nations without eVisa or a visa-free policy may receive a visa. To prevent any possible annoyance or delays at the airport, it is normally advised to get the e-Visa in advance.

Visa necessary: People from nations that do not fit into any of the categories listed above will normally need a visa to enter Azerbaijan. They must submit a visa application at the closest embassy or consulate of Azerbaijan in their place of residence. Depending on the place of origin, different regulations and processes could apply.

Visa Categories

There are several visa types available in Baku, the capital of Azerbaijan, for various travel reasons. The visa categories in Baku are designed to meet the requirements of visitors, business travelers, students, and those looking for work or permanent residence in the nation. The following is a thorough explanation of several popular visa types in Baku:

Tourist Visa: Those who want to go to Azerbaijan for pleasure, sightseeing, or to meet friends and relatives should apply for a tourist visa. It permits a short-term stay of up to 30 days within the nation. Azerbaijani embassies and consulates overseas, as well as online visa application platforms, provide tourist visas.

Business Visa: Those who want to conduct business-related activities in Azerbaijan should apply for a business visa. This involves going to conferences, meetings, talks, or looking at business possibilities. A stay of up to 90 days is permitted with a business visa, which is available for single or multiple entries and 180-day stays.

Student Visa: Those who want to study at a higher level in Azerbaijan must apply for a student visa. An acceptance letter from an accredited educational institution in Azerbaijan is required for this visa category. Typically, student visas are granted for the length of the academic program and may be renewed for further terms.

Work Visa: Those who have a job lined up in Azerbaijan must apply for a work visa. The applicant must provide the required paperwork, including an employment contract and credentials verification, and the employer in Azerbaijan must support the visa application. According to the terms of the employment contract, work visas are provided for a set duration and may be renewed.

A resident permit enables people to stay in Azerbaijan for a prolonged length of time. It is often acquired after arriving in the nation on an appropriate visa, such as a work or student visa. For people wishing to remain in Azerbaijan for extended periods, such as expatriate employees, retirees, or those looking to reunite with family, residence permits are necessary.

Transit Visa: If you are traveling via Baku and won't be leaving the airport's international transit area, you may be free from needing a transit visa. A transit visa must be obtained, nevertheless, if you want to leave the airport or remain for a long time.

Visa Application Process

Azerbaijan's capital city of Baku's visa application process includes some processes and conditions. The steps involved in applying for a visa to Baku are listed below in detail:

Determine the Type of Visa You Need: Based on the reason for your travel, you must first determine the type of visa you need. There are several different types of visas available in Azerbaijan, including transit, business, student, and tourist visas. Choose the correct visa type since each category has unique criteria and stays limited.

After determining the sort of visa you want, gather all the paperwork you'll need to apply. Depending on your nationality and visa category, the specific criteria could change. However, usually speaking, the following paperwork is required:

A passport must be valid for at least six months beyond the expected length of stay in Azerbaijan.
Fill out the visa application form completely, clearly, and concisely. This form may be located at the embassy or consulate of Azerbaijan on your nation's website.
pictures of the size of a passport: Include current, color pictures of the size of a passport with your application. Check the precise specifications since they could differ, such as size and backdrop color.

You could need an invitation letter from a host in Azerbaijan depending on the reason for your visit. A business invitation, for instance, is necessary if you're seeking a business visa.

Proof of lodging: Submit documentation attesting to your accommodations for the duration of your visit to Baku. If you are staying with relatives or friends, this might be a letter of invitation from your hosts or hotel bookings.

Flight itinerary: Hand along a copy of your confirmed round-trip tickets or a thorough itinerary that includes the dates of your arrival and departure.

Financial records: Present evidence that you have enough money to meet your costs while you are in Azerbaijan. This may be shown by bank records, letters of support, or a letter from your company outlining your pay and leave details.

Obtain travel insurance that includes coverage for unexpected medical costs and other emergencies during your visit to Azerbaijan.

Application Submission: After gathering all necessary documentation, send your application to the Azerbaijani embassy or consulate that is most conveniently located in your nation. The ASAN Visa site also allows applicants in certain nations to submit their applications online. To avoid any delays, be sure to submit your application long before the dates you want to travel.

Pay the Visa charge: Depending on your nationality and visa category, you may also be required to pay a visa charge. Please verify the embassy or consulate's particular regulations since the payment method may vary. Keep in mind that even if your application is rejected, visa payments are often non-refundable.

Attend the visa interview (if necessary): The Azerbaijani embassy or consulate may sometimes ask you to come in for a visa interview so they may review your application in more detail. If this is necessary, make an appointment and be ready to discuss your itinerary, money, and other pertinent information.

Track the Application: Using the reference number you were given after submitting your application, you may keep tabs on its development. You may use this to keep track of the progress of your visa application.

Obtaining the Visa: The embassy or consulate will inform you when your visa application is granted. For your visa, go to the embassy or consulate. Verify the visa's validity dates and other information to make sure they correspond with your trip schedule.

It is important to note that the procedure for applying for a visa may differ significantly depending on your nationality, thus it is advised to examine the particular prerequisites and guidelines provided by the Azerbaijani embassy or consulate in your country.

Evidence of Sufficient Funding

To describe the proof of adequate cash in Baku, Azerbaijan, in-depth, it is necessary to take into account the specifications and procedures that are normally followed for various tasks, such as visa applications or bank transactions. Here is a list of such typical situations:

Application for a visa

Applicants are sometimes needed to provide proof that they have enough money to pay their expenditures throughout their stay to get a visa to visit Azerbaijan. This is done to make sure that tourists are financially independent and won't burden their host nation. Depending on the objective and length of the visit, a different quantity may be needed.

Applicants may normally present the following records as proof of enough funds:

Original or certified bank statements over the last three to six months that indicate a positive account balance. The remaining balance should show enough money to pay for any scheduled activities, lodging, travel, and meals.

Invitation or Sponsorship Letters: If someone else is paying for the trip, they may need to provide a sponsorship letter indicating their readiness to pay the applicant's expenditures as well as supporting documentation of their financial capability.

Traveler's checks or Cash: As an extra means of demonstrating financial capabilities, it may be beneficial to carry traveler's checks or show access to a sufficient quantity of cash.

Salary Slips or Employment Letter: For those who are currently working, supplying recent salary slips or an employment letter outlining the person's job, pay, and length of employment will bolster their assertion of financial stability.

Company paperwork: For self-employed people or company owners, showing pertinent business paperwork, including registration documents, tax returns, or business bank records, may verify their financial reliability.

Financial Exchanges:
Some financial procedures, like establishing a bank account or making large purchases, could also call for proof of adequate finances. The specific procedures and requirements may vary across banks and institutions, but generally speaking, the following papers are often required:

a) Bank Statements: Current bank statements that typically span the previous three to six months and show a constant balance that satisfies the necessary standards.

b) Income Proof: Evidence of income, such as pay stubs, tax returns, or company financial statements, to confirm a consistent and reliable source of income.

c) Investment Documentation: If the money came from investments, you may provide proof by showing your stock holdings, ownership of real estate, or investment account statements.

d) Property value: A property value report or pertinent ownership documentation may be needed in certain circumstances when the owner of real estate is cited as evidence of funding.

e) Letter of Intent: A letter describing the rationale for the transaction and the intended use of the money might support the assertion that there is a need for the cash.

It's vital to keep in mind that the particular criteria and paperwork may change based on the situation, the institution or embassy involved, and the objective of the necessity for the proof of adequate finances. It is always advised to get the most current and recent information on the particular requirements in Baku, Azerbaijan, from the appropriate authorities or institutions.

Vaccinations

To guarantee a safe and healthy journey, it's crucial to be informed of the necessary immunizations before traveling to Baku. While I can provide you with some broad information, it's important to speak with a doctor or travel medicine expert for tailored guidance based on your particular health issues, vaccination records, and travel plans. Additionally, vaccine requirements might vary over time, so it's important to keep current by consulting reputable sources like the World Health Organization (WHO) or the Centers for Disease Control and Prevention (CDC).

The following vaccines are often advised for visitors to Baku:
Ensure that you are up to date on standard vaccines such as those for influenza, polio, diphtheria, tetanus, rubella

(MMR), and diphtheria, tetanus, and pertussis (DTaP). These shots guard against common infections and are often advised regardless of travel plans.

Hepatitis A: Contaminated food and water may spread the virus that causes hepatitis A. It is strongly advised for the majority of visitors to Baku since there may be a danger of exposure in particular regions or from ingesting local cuisine and beverages. The vaccination normally requires two doses, spaced at least six months apart, and offers long-term protection.

Hepatitis B is a viral illness that may be spread through blood, intercourse, or infected needles. The vaccination is advised for tourists who could interact closely with the local populace, need medical treatment, or participate in activities that might expose them to blood or bodily fluids. Over six months, the vaccination is given in a series of three doses.

Typhoid Fever: A bacterial illness, typhoid fever is spread through tainted food and water. Visitors to regions with subpar sanitation and hygiene standards run the risk of becoming sick. Depending on the vaccination type used, a booster dose may be necessary every two to five years. The vaccine may be given orally or by injection.

The viral illness rabies is spread through the bite or scratch of infected animals like dogs, bats, or monkeys. The vaccination should be taken into consideration by travelers who want to participate in outdoor activities or have frequent contact with animals. Three doses of the immunization are given over a month, and extra doses could be necessary if there is a chance of exposure.

Meningococcal illness is a bacterial infection that may lead to sepsis and meningitis. It is advised for tourists who could interact with locals for an extended period or take part in busy places or sizable gatherings, such as festivals or pilgrimages. There are many meningococcal disease vaccinations available, such as quadrivalent and serogroup B vaccines.

Please keep in mind that this list is not all-inclusive and that extra immunizations may be suggested for you, based on your situation. Additionally, it's critical to practice basic hand hygiene, drink clean water, consume food that's been properly prepared, and avoid mosquito bites by using insect repellents and using protective clothes.

In any event, it is strongly advised that you speak with a medical professional or travel medicine expert well in advance of your trip to Baku to ensure you get the most precise and recent advice on vaccines and health precautions for your particular requirements.

Chapter 3: Accommodation and Price Options

Hotels and Resort on a Budget

While Baku is home to several opulent hotels, it also has some budget-friendly lodging options that provide pleasant stays without breaking the bank. The following is a thorough summary of Baku's inexpensive hotels and resorts:

Sahil Hostel & Hotel is a low-cost lodging choice for visitors and is situated in the center of Baku. It provides tidy, comfortable accommodations with standard features like free Wi-Fi, air conditioning, and private bathrooms. A shared kitchen, laundry facilities, and a front desk are also available at the hostel. Due to its strategic position, major attractions, dining options, and public transit are all easily accessible.

Atropat Hotel: This low-cost hotel, which is located in Baku's Old City, provides cozy rooms at reasonable rates. The accommodations, which include air conditioning, satellite TV, and private toilets, are basic but well-maintained. The hotel has free Wi-Fi, room service, and a 24-hour front desk. Visitors may tour the nearby historic sites and landmarks because of their handy location.

Budget-friendly Premier Hotel is a lodging choice in Baku's Nasimi neighborhood. The hotel provides tidy, contemporary rooms with flat-screen TVs, cozy mattresses, and private bathrooms. Free Wi-Fi, a complimentary breakfast, and access to a fitness facility are available to visitors. The Premier Hotel is a great option for guests on a tight budget since it has excellent access to the city center through public transit.

Irshad Hotel: Located in the Sabayil neighborhood, Irshad Hotel offers budget-friendly lodging with a variety of features. Although the accommodations are basic, they include private bathrooms, air conditioning, and flat-screen televisions. The hotel has free Wi-Fi, a complimentary breakfast, and a round-the-clock front desk. Popular destinations including Fountain Square and the Heydar Aliyev Center are nearby.

Sahil Inn Hotel: Located close to Baku Boulevard, Sahil Inn Hotel provides inexpensive lodging with cozy rooms and contemporary conveniences. The rooms provide satellite TV, air conditioning, and private bathrooms. The hotel has complimentary Wi-Fi, a 24-hour front desk, and several breakfast selections. It's a great option for vacationers on a tight budget because of its proximity to the waterfront and sights like Maiden Tower and the Carpet Museum.

The Nasimi neighborhood's Four Season Hostel is a low-cost lodging choice with both private rooms and dormitory-style accommodations. The hostel has lockers, common toilets, and tidy, comfy mattresses. Free Wi-Fi, a shared kitchen, and comfortable common space are available to guests. The Four Season Hostel's prime location close to transit options makes exploring Baku's attractions simple.

These are just a few instances of reasonably priced hotels and resorts in Baku. It is advised to check online booking services and read reviews while looking for inexpensive lodging to locate the finest choice that fits your needs and price range. When making your choice, keep things like location, facilities, and closeness to attractions in mind.

Luxury Hotels and Resorts

Baku, a well-liked tourist destination, has a selection of opulent lodging options for the discriminating visitor. These places provide top-notch facilities, first-rate service, and beautiful vistas to make for an experience that will never be forgotten. Let's look at some of Baku's most upscale resorts and hotels.

The Four Seasons Hotel Baku provides a mix of contemporary luxury and classic elegance. It is centrally located in the city. The hotel offers suites and rooms with generous space, a sophisticated design, opulent decor, and cutting-edge services. The hotel's restaurants and bars provide a variety of eating choices, including both international cuisine and regional specialties. Offering a range of restorative treatments, the spa and wellness center offers a peaceful refuge. Visitors may take in breathtaking views of the city and the sea thanks to the hotel's excellent position on the Caspian Sea beachfront.

Located in the renowned Flame Towers complex, the Fairmont Baku provides an opulent refuge with sweeping views of the city and the Caspian Sea. The hotel offers generously sized guest rooms and suites with opulent furnishings, modern design, and high-end services. In the hotel's restaurants, a variety of foreign and Azerbaijani cuisines are available for guests to sample. A variety of treatments and health amenities, including an indoor pool, are offered by the spa and fitness center. The hotel's position also makes it simple to reach Baku's top sights.

JW Marriott Absheron Baku: This popular hotel is known for its upscale decor and first-rate service. It is conveniently located in the heart of the city. The hotel provides opulent lodging options, including sizable rooms and suites with classy furnishings and contemporary conveniences. At the hotel's restaurants, which provide a blend of foreign and Azerbaijani cuisine, guests may go on a gastronomic trip. Views of the downtown skyline are stunning from the rooftop terrace and bar. A rooftop pool is one of the amenities offered by the spa and wellness center of the hotel.

Jumeirah Bilgah Beach Hotel: Jumeirah Bilgah Beach Hotel provides an opulent beachfront experience and is located on the scenic beaches of the Caspian Sea. The hotel's elegantly built villas, suites, and rooms provide a calm, refined ambiance. From informal seaside cafés to gourmet dining establishments serving foreign cuisine, visitors may choose from a wide variety of eating experiences. A wonderful and restful stay is guaranteed with the hotel's beach, swimming pools, and water sports facilities. For the utmost relaxation, the spa and wellness center offers a range of therapies and treatments.

Hilton Baku: Conveniently situated in the heart of the city, Hilton Baku provides opulent modern comfort and first-rate service. The hotel offers chic, luxurious guest rooms and suites with breathtaking views of the city or the Caspian Sea. The hotel's restaurants, which offer a range of cuisines, including dishes from Azerbaijan, invite visitors to go on a gastronomic adventure. Cocktails may be enjoyed in front of a magnificent background at the rooftop bar and lounge. The hotel also has a spa, indoor pool, and fitness center for visitors to relax and refresh.

These opulent resorts and hotels in Baku provide a remarkable combination of convenience, style, and first-rate service. They are the epitome of extravagance. These places provide a refuge of luxury and indulgence, providing an exceptional stay in the dynamic city of Baku, whether visitors are there for business or pleasure.

Vacation Rentals and Apartments

Baku is a thriving city that is continually growing. It is renowned for its beautiful architecture, rich history, and cultural legacy. Baku, a well-known tourist destination, provides a variety of lodging choices, including flats and rental homes, to satisfy the requirements and tastes of guests.

Apartments in Baku: Both short-term and long-term stays are common in this city's apartments. With greater room and facilities than standard hotel rooms, they provide a cozy and practical home away from home. Baku offers a wide variety of flats, from chic new high-rise structures to quaint historic townhouses.

Location: Visitors have the option to choose an apartment that is located in a neighborhood that best matches their needs among those available around the city. For those seeking to be in the center of the city, downtown Baku is a popular option because of its busy streets, malls, and cultural attractions. Other areas, such as the Seafront, Fountain Square, and the Old City (Icheri Sheher), provide distinctive experiences with convenient access to historical landmarks, dining options, and nightlife.

Apartments in Baku are available in a range of sizes, from comfortable studios to roomy multi-bedroom residences. They often come with all of the necessary furnishings and conveniences, including cozy bedrooms, living rooms, kitchens or kitchenettes, and private bathrooms. Additionally, larger apartments could provide extra amenities like balconies, washers, WiFi, and air conditioning. Before making a reservation, it's crucial to confirm the precise facilities offered by each property.

Booking Sites: A variety of websites and rental companies provide a large range of flats in Baku. Popular platforms include local vacation rental websites, Booking.com, and Airbnb. To assist users in making educated judgments, these platforms include thorough explanations, top-notch images, and user reviews.

Vacation rentals are available in Baku in addition to apartments, and are designed with visitors and travelers in mind. For those looking for a distinctive and immersive experience during their visit to the city, vacation rentals are perfect. Key characteristics of Baku holiday rentals include the following:

Unique Properties: Baku vacation rentals often feature homes like villas, cottages, and the traditional "chardags" of Azerbaijan. These buildings are intended to provide a particular ambiance and showcase the architectural and cultural traditions of the area.

Recreational Facilities: Additional features and recreational amenities like private gardens, swimming pools, saunas, and gyms may be included in vacation rentals. These amenities provide possibilities for leisure and amusement while also enhancing the entire holiday experience.

Local Attractions: Locals who are enthusiastic about presenting their culture and traditions own and operate several holiday properties in Baku. They could provide specialized services like private excursions, culinary lessons, and cultural encounters to let guests fully experience the way of life in the area.

Booking and Availability: You may reserve a vacation rental in Baku through a variety of websites and neighborhood rental companies. To guarantee the preferred property and dates, it is preferable to make reservations in advance, particularly during busy travel times.

Both apartment living and holiday rentals in Baku provide freedom, privacy, and a pleasant living environment, enabling you to make the most of your time in this alluring city.

Campouts and Glamping

Outdoor lovers may experience nature in Baku while still living comfortably and opulently via glamping and camping. Baku offers the ideal environment for both glamping and conventional camping because of its fascinating history, breathtaking scenery, and varied cultural heritage.

Glamping in Baku: Glamping, which combines the words "glamorous" and "camping," takes the idea of basic camping and adds opulent facilities and luxuries. Travelers who want a more upscale outdoor experience may discover a variety of glamping locations in Baku that provide a choice of cozy and fashionable alternatives.

Glamping venues in Baku include a range of lodging options, such as deluxe tents, yurts, eco-cabins, and treehouses. These lodgings often provide nice bedding, electricity, heating and cooling systems, private bathrooms, and sometimes even Wi-Fi.

Glamping locations in Baku provide a variety of services and amenities to make your stay more enjoyable. On-site dining establishments providing delectable regional cuisine, swimming pools, spa treatments, hot tubs, social gathering places, and sometimes even planned activities or guided tours are among the facilities you may anticipate.

Beautiful surroundings: There are a lot of glamping locations in Baku that provide breathtaking views of the surrounding natural landscapes, including mountains, woods, and lakes. These picturesque areas provide a calm and quiet ambiance that enables visitors to connect with nature while taking a luxury escape.

Baku and its surroundings provide a wide variety of campgrounds that appeal to outdoor enthusiasts for those who want a more conventional camping experience. Camping in Baku enables you to experience the simplicity of outdoor life, get close to nature, and discover the natural treasures of the area.

Camping: There are some campgrounds in and around Baku, ranging from simple sites with few amenities to more developed campgrounds with more amenities. While some campgrounds could provide pre-pitched tents for hire, other campsites include dedicated areas for tents, campers, or caravans.

Camping places in Baku often provide communal restrooms with toilets and showers, cooking areas with fire pits or BBQ grills, picnic tables, and sometimes even little convenience shops. The particular facilities provided at each campground must be confirmed in advance, however, since they might differ.

Camping in Baku allows you to enjoy the area's natural beauties, including the breathtaking Gobustan National Park, which is renowned for its historic rock carvings and distinctive mud volcanoes. You may also go to the Absheron Peninsula to take in the picturesque Caspian Sea shoreline or explore the neighboring highlands for options for climbing and trekking.

Outdoor Activities: Baku camping offers a great chance to participate in a variety of outdoor activities. You may go birding, hiking, fishing, or just unwind by the campfire and gaze at the stars. Additionally, some campgrounds have planned activities including off-road excursions, horseback riding, and guided nature hikes.

Whether you prefer glamping or conventional camping, Baku provides a stunning fusion of the outdoors, history, and contemporary conveniences. It's a place that welcomes both thrill-seekers and those seeking a more opulent outdoor experience, enabling guests to make priceless memories in the capital city of Azerbaijan.

Chapter 4: Acceptable Étiquettes and NightLife

There are a few things to remember to have a nice experience when it comes to being polite and taking advantage of Baku's nightlife. Here is a thorough explanation of appropriate behavior and the Baku nighttime scene:

Dress Code: People in Baku tend to dress in a variety of ways due to the city's relatively lax dress code. When going to upscale clubs, pubs, or restaurants, it is suggested to wear somewhat more formal attire. In most places, casual clothing is okay, but it's always a good idea to dress formally so you fit in.

Being on time for appointments or scheduled activities is considered courteous since Azerbaijanis place a high emphasis on punctuality. This is true whether going out to eat, seeing a performance, or seeing friends. Being on time allows you to completely appreciate the event and demonstrates respect for other people's time.

Reservations are advised since Baku's nightlife may grow hectic, particularly on weekends. Therefore, it is wise to arrange reservations in advance, especially for well-known locations or exclusive clubs. This guarantees you space and protects you from disappointment if a location is completely booked.

Socializing & Interactions: In general, Azerbaijanis are kind and hospitable. In pubs and clubs, it's typical to start up a discussion with both locals and other guests. While nice talk is welcomed, it's crucial to respect others' privacy and avoid being unduly invasive or hurtful.

Tipping: In restaurants, pubs, and nightclubs around Baku, tipping is usual and often expected. It is customary to tip between 10% and 15% of the entire cost. However, because some places do add a service fee to the bill, it's always a good idea to double-check.

Nightlife Locations: Baku has a wide variety of nightlife locations to suit all interests and preferences. Everything from hip pubs and clubs to live music venues, lounges, and rooftop bars can be found here. The city's core, Fountain Square, Nizami Street, and the seaside promenade are among the hotspots for nightlife. It is best to do your homework and choose locations depending on your tastes and the kind of experience you want.

Safety: Although Baku is a generally safe city, it's always advisable to use care and pay attention to your surroundings, particularly when taking in the city's nightlife. Travel with dependable friends, stay in well-lit, busy locations, and refrain from taking beverages from random people. Using authorized taxis or ride-sharing services is advised while navigating the city at night.

Alcohol Consumption: Baku has a thriving nightlife with several establishments providing alcoholic drinks. It's important to drink sensibly and to be conscious of your intake. To protect your safety and the pleasure of the evening, it is advised to maintain a modest level of alcohol intake. Public drunkenness is often frowned upon.

Baku's nightlife often consists of dancing and music. Live bands, DJs, and dance acts are often included in clubs and pubs. If you feel comfortable doing so, feel free to participate in the dancing, but always be considerate of others' privacy and happiness.

Closing Time: On weekdays, nightlife establishments in Baku typically shut at 2:00 am, but on weekends, they do so around 4:00 am. To guarantee a seamless exit from the event, it is advised to plan your evening appropriately and to make travel plans.

Dress Tips for Men

With a blend of traditional and contemporary designs, Baku is renowned for its dynamic and diversified fashion scene. To assist you navigate Baku's fashion scene, consider the following advice regarding men's attire:

Baku has a semi-arid climate with scorching summers and moderate winters, so dress appropriately. The summer months (June to August) may be quite hot, so choose breathable materials with a light touch, like linen or cotton. It may become cold throughout the winter (December to February), so it's best to layer with a coat or jacket.

Smart-casual dress is suited for the majority of situations in the cosmopolitan metropolis of Baku. Choose well-fitted chinos, dark jeans, or chinos to go with a chic shirt or polo shirt. For a more professional appearance, add a blazer or fitted jacket to the outfit.

Traditional attire: For formal events or cultural occasions, you may choose to wear traditional Azerbaijani clothing, such as a national costume called "chokha" or a long coat known as "arkhalig." These clothes are frequently embellished with intricate embroidery and can add a touch of elegance to your outfit.

Footwear: For visiting the city, you must have comfortable but fashionable shoes. Choose open-toed sandals or loafers in the summer, and closed-toed shoes or boots in the fall and winter. Since Baku's streets are generally kept up nicely, wearing leather shoes is generally safe.

Pay attention to your accessories since they may make your clothing seem better. For more formal events, think about donning a fashionable watch, a belt that matches your attire, and maybe a pocket square or tie. Sunglasses are a useful item to have if you want to shield your eyes from the sun.

Being sensitive to cultural differences is crucial since Azerbaijan is a nation with a large Muslim population. Although Baku is a liberal city, it is nonetheless advised to dress modestly, particularly when visiting places of worship or going to formal events. Do not dress provocatively or revealingly.

Colors and patterns: A broad variety of colors and designs are used in Baku's fashion industry. Don't be afraid to include more striking colors like royal blue, burgundy, or emerald green in your wardrobe. While neutral colors like black, gray, and navy are usually safe options, don't limit yourself to these. To add interest to your clothing, try experimenting with patterns like checks, stripes, or subtle designs.

Grooming: Pay attention to your grooming as it might improve how you look. Maintain a tidy hairstyle, clip your nails, and, if you have facial hair, groom it. If you want expert assistance, there are several barbershops and grooming facilities in Baku.

Keep in mind that these are basic guidelines, and the appropriate attire may change based on the event or location you're going to. To make sure you're dressed suitably, it's always a good idea to check the dress codes ahead of time or to look at what the locals are wearing.

Dress Tips for Women

Baku is a bustling, international metropolis with a blend of ancient and contemporary architecture. Here are some suggestions to help you look presentable and respectable in Baku:

Respect the Culture: Although Baku is more liberal than rural regions given that Azerbaijan is primarily a Muslim nation, it is nevertheless important to dress modestly out of respect for the people's customs and culture. Avoid wearing anything too exposing, especially in places where people are conservative or religious.

Choose Lightweight Textiles: Due to Baku's scorching summers, it's important to use lightweight, breathable textiles while dressing. Choose fabrics made of natural fibers that promote airflow and help to drain perspiration away, such as cotton, linen, or light mixes.

Embrace Stylish Yet Conservative Attire: By selecting stylish apparel, you may still express your style while dressing modestly. Choose dresses, skirts, or pants that are knee-length or longer. Sleeves and the neckline of tops should cover your shoulders. When it's warm outside, loose-fitting clothes are often a wise option for comfort.

Azerbaijan has a rich cultural background, thus it's important to take cultural sensitivity into account while choosing your clothing. This may be accomplished by adorning traditional Azerbaijani jewelry or by dressing in regional patterns and styles.

Be Prepared for Variable Weather: Layering your clothing is a good idea since Baku's weather may change quickly. Carry a lightweight jacket, shawl, or cardigan in case the weather cools down at night or if you want to visit an establishment with air conditioning, such as a mall or restaurant.

The best footwear should be used since Baku is a city that necessitates a decent bit of walking. Choose fashionable but useful footwear like flats, sneakers, or sandals. Unless you are going to a formal occasion or a luxury restaurant, stay away from wearing uncomfortable shoes or high heels.

Respectful Swimwear: If you want to visit Baku's beaches or swimming pools, choose modest swimwear that suitably covers your body. Even while certain private clubs or beaches can have more permissive regulations, it's always best to err on the side of caution and wear swimwear that respects the local way of life.

Wear something fancy for nighttime excursions since Baku has a thriving nightlife. Select classy shirts to go with dresses, skirts, or fitted bottoms. It's common for Baku inhabitants to dress up for nighttime gatherings, so don't be shy about embracing avant-garde fashion.

Consider the Mosque Dress Code: It's necessary to observe the dress code while visiting mosques in Baku. Women should avoid wearing exposing apparel, cover their legs and arms with loose-fitting clothing, and cover their heads with scarves.

Remember that the goal of these dressing suggestions is to help you fit in with the community and respect Baku's customs. Feel free to exhibit your style while adhering to these rules and taking advantage of the city's thriving fashion scene.

Food

The rich, varied, and deeply ingrained cultural legacy of Azerbaijan is reflected in the cuisine of the nation. When visiting Baku, try these popular dishes:

Plov: In Azerbaijani cuisine, plov is a classic rice dish that is highly regarded. It comprises meat (often lamb or chicken) and a variety of fragrant spices cooked with delicate rice and saffron. Dried fruits and nuts, as well as sometimes caramelized onions, enhance the taste. Plov is a standard dish served at weddings and other special events.

Dolma is a well-known delicacy fashioned from grape leaves or vegetables like bell peppers or tomatoes that have been filled with a blend of ground beef, rice, herbs, and spices. After being cooked until soft, the dolma is then served with yogurt or a sauce made of tomatoes. It's a tasty and filling meal that highlights the tastes and artistry of Azerbaijani cuisine.

Kebabs: These skewered meat delicacies are created using different types of lamb, beef, or chicken, and are a national delicacy of Azerbaijan. Sumac, saffron, and cumin are among the spices used to marinade the meat before it is grilled over open flames to perfection. As a consequence, juicy, tender kebabs with a smokey taste are produced.

Dushbara: This heart-warming Azerbaijani soup is a staple dish. It comprises miniature dumplings, usually served in a savory soup, that are stuffed with ground lamb or beef. The tiny, delicate dumplings resemble miniature tortellini in size. Dushbara is often served with a dollop of yogurt and topped with fresh herbs like cilantro or dill.

Lavash: Lavash is an important ingredient in Azerbaijani cuisine. It is a soft, thin, unleavened bread. Usually cooked in a tandoor (clay oven), it is a side dish for many different cuisines. Lavash may be split into pieces and dipped in savory sauces and spreads like hummus or dips made with eggplant. It can also be used to wrap kebabs, dolma, or plov.

Pakhlava: If you have a sweet craving, try this classic Azerbaijani delicacy. Layers of thin pastry dough are used to create it, and within are mixtures of crushed nuts, sugar, and spices like cardamom or cinnamon. The pastry is then cooked before being dipped into a honey or sugary syrup to create a sweet syrup with a flaky texture.

Tea is a significant element of social events and has a specific position in Azerbaijani culture. Make sure to attend a traditional tea ceremony if you visit Baku. Azerbaijani tea, which is normally black and powerful, is frequently served with a cube of sugar or a tablespoon of homemade jam in little pear-shaped cups known as "armudu." An assortment of pastries and sweets are often served with tea.

These are just a handful of the amazing Azerbaijani cuisine highlights that you may experience while in Baku. There are many lively marketplaces, tea shops, and restaurants around the city where you may enjoy the tastes and scents of this extensive culinary culture. Don't pass up the chance to savor these delectable delicacies and discover Baku's culinary delights.

Drinks

The regional beverages follow the tradition of Azerbaijani cuisine, which is renowned for its complex tastes and unusual pairings. When visiting Baku, you should try the following beverages:

Ayran: In Azerbaijan and many other nations in the area, ayran is a well-liked traditional beverage. To make it, combine yogurt, water, and a dash of salt. A cool, somewhat salty, and tangy beverage is the end product, which is ideal for soothing thirst, particularly on hot summer days.

Dovga: Dovga is a classic yogurt-based soup and beverage from Azerbaijan. Fermented yogurt, rice, herbs (such as spinach, coriander, and dill), and sometimes chickpeas are used to make it. Dovga is often served cold and has a creamy texture and acidic flavor. Try it while you're in Baku; it's a distinctive and healthy beverage.

Sherbet is a well-liked sweet drink in Azerbaijan that is often offered at festive events. Fruit juices (such as pomegranate, cherry, or mulberry) are combined with water, sugar, and other ingredients to create them. Dried fruit and nuts are often used as sherbet garnishes because they enhance the dessert's taste and texture.

Black tea is the most widely consumed kind of tea in Azerbaijan, a country with a rich tea-drinking tradition. The tea is often prepared in a samovar, a vintage tea kettle, and served in little armudu cups, which lack handles. Because of its robust taste, Azerbaijani tea is sometimes paired with a sugar cube or a tablespoon of homemade jam.

Sahlab: Made from milk and orchid tubers, sahlab is a warm, creamy beverage. It has a thick, velvety texture and is flavored with things like rosewater, cinnamon, and occasionally nuts. On chilly days, sahlab is a warming beverage that will keep you warm.

Pomegranate juice: Pomegranates are renowned in Azerbaijan, and you can easily find delicious fresh pomegranate juice in Baku. This vibrant red juice is full of antioxidants and is both cooling and healthy. If you enjoy fruity and tangy drinks, you must try it.

Araq is a traditional alcoholic beverage from Azerbaijan that is frequently referred to as the country's favorite. It is a fermented fruit spirit that is typically made from grapes or mulberries and is distilled. The flavor of araq is strong and distinctive, akin to that of vodka or brandy. It may be drunk either straight or diluted with water during festive events.

Turkish coffee is available at numerous cafés and restaurants, despite Baku not being historically recognized as a coffee city. Turkic coffee is robust, thick, and fragrant and is often served in tiny glasses. A glass of water is typically served with it to refresh the palate in between bites.

These are just a few of the beverages you ought to sample while in Baku. You can fully immerse yourself in Azerbaijani culinary traditions by sampling each one, which offers a distinctive flavor and cultural experience. Baku has a drink to suit every taste, whether you prefer cool non-alcoholic beverages or want to try the regional spirits.

Street Food and Snacks

Baku offers a thriving street food scene that highlights the nation's extensive culinary history. Here are some must-try street delicacies and snacks that will excite your taste buds:

Dushbara: Dushbara are little, dumpling-like delicacies that are a mainstay of Azerbaijani cuisine. These little dumplings are frequently packed with minced meat and herbs and cooked in a delicious broth. Dushbara is commonly served with a dollop of yogurt or sour cream and sprinkled with sumac for an added acidic flavor. They make for a cozy and excellent street food choice.

Qutab: Qutab is a popular Azerbaijani flatbread that comes with different fillings. The dough is rolled thin, filled with ingredients such as minced meat, herbs, cheese, or pumpkin, and then grilled on a hot griddle until crispy. Qutab is commonly folded or rolled and served hot, making it a handy and delectable street food snack.

Döner kebab: Although originating from Turkey, döner kebab has become a beloved street food dish in Baku. Slices of marinated meat, often lamb or chicken, are gently roasted on a vertical spit, then thinly sliced and served on warm pita bread. It is commonly complemented by fresh vegetables, herbs, and savory sauces. You'll find döner kebab vendors throughout the city, particularly in busier places and near tourist attractions.

Baklava: For those with a sweet craving, Baklava is a must-try dessert. This decadent dessert consists of layers of thin, flaky pastry filled with a variety of finely chopped nuts, such as almonds, walnuts, or pistachios, and sweetened with honey or syrup. Baklava is rich and delicious, making it the ideal finish to a street food journey in Baku.

Samsa: Samsa is a wonderful baked pastry that is famous in Azerbaijan. It is akin to a samosa or a triangular-shaped turnover. The dough is frequently filled with minced meat, onions, and spices, then baked until golden and crispy. Samsa is commonly eaten as a fast snack, and you'll find it in numerous street food booths and bakeries in Baku.

Pakhlava: Another wonderful Azerbaijani delicacy is pakhlava. It is a delicious pastry created with layers of thin dough, lavishly loaded with ground nuts, sugar, and aromatic spices such as cardamom or cinnamon. The pastry is then fried till brown and served with a sweet syrup sprinkled on top. Pakhlava is a wonderful dessert that highlights the region's affinity for sweet tastes.

While touring Baku, be sure to taste these street food and snack alternatives to thoroughly immerse yourself in the city's culinary traditions.

Best Eateries and Coffee Shops

Baku is home to a large number of excellent restaurants and cafés that accommodate a range of tastes and preferences, from traditional Azerbaijani cuisine to cosmopolitan delicacies. The following is a thorough overview of some of the city's top eateries:

Featuring a sumptuous dining experience and stunning views of the Caspian Sea, Baku's Firuze Restaurant is ideally situated in the city center. The restaurant provides a variety of meals made with fresh and regional ingredients and specializes in Azerbaijani cuisine. Traditional staples including kebabs, plov (rice pilaf), and dolma (stuffed grape leaves) are skilfully prepared to offer true tastes.

Chinar Restaurant: Located on the well-known Baku Boulevard, Chinar Restaurant offers a menu that highlights the finest of Azerbaijani and world cuisine in an opulent setting. A posh environment is created by the restaurant's exquisite setting, which includes crystal chandeliers and attractive furnishings. Every appetite may be appeased by the variety of foods offered by Chinar Restaurant, which includes fresh seafood, exquisite grilled meats, and vegetarian alternatives.

The Nargiz Restaurant is well known for its welcoming atmosphere and superb Azerbaijani hospitality. An intimate eating experience is created by the warm and welcoming ambiance that is decorated with traditional Azerbaijani elements. There are several traditional meals on the menu, including shah pilaf (a fragrant rice dish), Qutab (savory pancakes), and dushbara (dumplings). The cultural mood is further enhanced by live traditional music performances.

Azerbaijani and Middle Eastern cuisines are combined at Sumakh Restaurant, which is located in Baku's famed

Old City. With exposed brick walls and wooden decorations, the restaurant has a rustic character that enhances its appeal. The cuisine at Sumakh features specialties including lamb kebabs, saffron-infused rice, and flavorful stews. It's the perfect place for a special dining experience because of the friendly service and lovely rooftop deck.

Paul's Bakery: If you're in the mood for some European food, you must go to Paul's Bakery. This quaint French bakery, which is situated in the heart of the city, serves a mouthwatering selection of freshly made bread, pastries, and cakes. The inviting ambiance is enhanced by the comforting scent of freshly baked products. Customers are delighted by the genuine French tastes of Paul's Bakery's flaky croissants and luscious macarons.

Passage 1901 is a chic eatery that combines European and Azerbaijani characteristics. It is housed in a beautifully renovated early 20th-century structure. A feeling of grandeur permeates the exquisite design, which has lofty ceilings and Art Nouveau details. The menu combines traditional European cuisine with Azerbaijani ingredients to produce creative and tasty meals. Passage 1901 offers a classy eating experience, whether it's for a work lunch or a special supper.

Sea Breeze Café provides a tranquil and attractive location for enjoying a meal or a cup of coffee. It is situated along the coastline of the Caspian Sea. While the quaint interior gives a welcoming ambiance, the outside terrace offers breathtaking views of the sea. Salads, sandwiches, and spaghetti are among the several foreign foods that are offered on the menu. The Sea Breeze Café is the perfect place to relax and enjoy Baku's seaside beauty.

Dining Manners

The dining manners of Baku, the capital of Azerbaijan, are a fusion of Central Asian, Middle Eastern, and Eastern European traditions. Here is a thorough explanation of Baku's eating manners:

Salutations and Courtesy:

It is normal to shake the host or hostess' hand while entering a restaurant or private residence. In more formal settings, males may even kiss the woman's hand.

Due to the wonderful hospitality of Azeris, it is typical for hosts to provide a wide selection of food and beverages to their visitors.

Seating Configuration:

In formal contexts, the sitting arrangement could correspond to a certain hierarchy or order of importance. Typically, the oldest or most distinguished visitor is placed at the head of the table.

As they could have a particular sitting arrangement, you should wait for the host or hostess to suggest where you should sit.

Table etiquette:

Table manners are often formal and courteous in Baku. Before starting your dinner, watch out for the host or hostess.

Slouching or placing your elbows on the table while eating is considered rude.

Avoid chatting while eating by chewing with your mouth shut.

Bread:

In Azerbaijani culture, bread is very important. Every meal often includes it.

It is polite to take a tiny piece and eat it before taking more, and it is usual to break the bread with your hands rather than a knife.

Utensils:

You could get a spoon and fork or a spoon and knife combo while dining in more traditional Azerbaijani establishments.

For soups and stews, one often uses a spoon, but for other foods, one typically uses a fork. Typically, the knife is used to cut meat and other things that need it.

Tea Consumption:

In Azerbaijan, tea is a common beverage that is often provided all day. As a gesture of hospitality, it is usual to provide tea to visitors.

grasp the cup by the handle when sipping tea, and it is customary to use the other hand to grasp the saucer.

You may put your hand over the cup to signal that you've had enough tea if you don't want anymore.

Alcohol and Toasts:

During meals, toasts are often made, particularly if alcohol is being drunk. The toasting customs of the Azeris are well recognized.

It is typical to stand up, hold your glass in one hand, and look the person you are toasting in the eye while making a toast.

Following a toast, it is customary to take a sip, although moderation is advised.

Tipping:

In Baku, tips are expected in restaurants and coffee shops. If you were pleased with the service, it's typical to tip between 10% and 15%.

Remember that although these suggestions might help you get a rough idea of Baku's eating traditions, they may change based on the situation or personal preferences. To make sure you are polite and thoughtful when eating in Baku, it is always essential to pay attention to and follow the example of your Azerbaijani hosts or the locals.

Chapter 5: Transportation Options and Costs in Baku

A variety of modes of transportation are available in Baku, the capital of Azerbaijan, to make getting about easier for locals and guests. Here is a thorough breakdown of the transportation choices offered in Baku, along with their prices, ranging from public transit to taxis and private automobile rentals:

Buses, the metro, and trams are all part of the large public transit system of Baku.

Buses

The whole city of Baku is serviced by a network of bus lines. Depending on the distance traveled, bus tickets typically range from 0.30 AZN (Azerbaijani Manat) to 0.50 AZN. When boarding the bus, tickets may be bought straight from the driver.

Subway

The Baku Within the city, the metro is a practical and effective mode of transportation. Three lines cover the majority of Baku's key regions. The metro runs from six in the morning till late. Regardless of the distance covered, the fee for a single journey is 0.20 AZN.

Trams

The city core of Baku is where the majority of the city's trams are located. Tram prices, which range from 0.30 to 0.50 AZN, are comparable to bus prices.

Taxis

A more flexible and convenient method to go about the city, taxis are a well-liked kind of transportation in Baku. There are two different categories of taxis:

Official Taxis: In Baku, official taxis are typically yellow and equipped with taximeters. You may either locate them at authorized taxi stands or hail them on the street since they are widely dispersed across the city. The first price is around 1 AZN, plus a fee for each extra kilometer.

Ride-Hailing Services

Uber and Bolt are two examples of ride-hailing apps that are accessible in Baku. With the help of these applications, you may order a taxi using your smartphone; the cost is determined by the distance covered. varying applications may charge somewhat varying prices, and there may be surge pricing during times of great demand.

Car Rentals

Car rentals are an additional means of getting about Baku. You may choose from a choice of automobiles depending on your preferences and spending limit from one of the many car rental firms that operate in the city. The cost of renting an automobile varies based on its model, length, and mileage allowance. A basic budget automobile will typically cost you between 50 and 80 AZN per day.

Walking and Bicycle

Walking and bicycling are both possible in Baku, especially in the city's center. Nearby restaurants, parks, and attractions are all easily accessible on foot. A cheap and entertaining method to see a city is by foot.

Bike-Sharing Schemes

Additionally, Baku has put in place bike-sharing schemes, and certain places even have specific bike lanes and bike stations. For a little cost, you may hire a bike and ride about the city.

More Options: Baku also has more transportation choices, including:

Flights between Nakhchivan and Baku: There are frequent flights between Nakhchivan and Baku. The flight lasts around an hour, and the price is determined by the airline and booking level.

The Baku International Bus Terminal provides long-distance bus services for those who want to go to other cities within Azerbaijan or to nearby nations. The cost of the tickets varies according to the bus class and the destination.

Train

Baku has a connection to the national rail network and provides train connections to some places both within and outside of Azerbaijan. The cost of the train varies according to the route taken and the class of the train.

Chapter 6: Essential tips you must know as a first Timer

Bring Some Cash with You

Though many businesses in Baku accept credit and debit cards, it is always a good idea to carry some cash when visiting. Here's why having cash on hand might be helpful and how much you might think about bringing:

Widespread Acceptance: Although card payments are becoming more widespread in Baku, it's crucial to keep in mind that not all establishments take cards, particularly in neighborhood markets, tiny stores, and certain modes of transportation. You may make sure you have the funds to make purchases of products, services, and experiences where card payments might not be accepted by keeping cash on hand.

Street Vendors & Local Markets: Baku is renowned for its thriving local markets, such as Taza Bazaar and Sharg Bazari, where you may buy a variety of fresh fruit, spices, gifts, and traditional crafts. Having local money will make shopping more convenient since many merchants in these marketplaces prefer cash payments.

Smaller establishments, such as family-run cafés and neighborhood restaurants, may offer fewer card payment alternatives than bigger retailers, upmarket restaurants, and chain hotels. Having cash on hand would enable you to enjoy the local food without any payment obstacles whether you want to explore Baku's diversified culinary scene or visit off-the-beaten-path eateries.

Buses, the metro, and taxis are just a few of the public transit choices available in Baku. Buses and taxis often demand cash, although metro cards may be bought and filled up with electronic payments. Cash may also be required if you want to go outside the city to see neighboring sites to pay for transportation costs or admission tickets.

Emergency Situations: Having some cash on hand is usually a smart precaution. It may be useful if unexpected events occur, such as a power outage that affects card terminals, network connection problems, or the need to pay for unanticipated charges that would not be payable by card.

In light of these elements, it is advised to travel with some cash while in Baku. Here are a few ideas:

a. The Azerbaijani Manat (AZN) is used as the country of Azerbaijan's official currency. Before leaving on your vacation, research exchange rates to see how much your native country's currency is worth.

b. Withdrawal: If you'd like to get cash locally, there are a ton of ATMs all across Baku where you may use your debit or credit card to get cash. However, to guarantee seamless overseas transactions, it's a good idea to let your bank know in advance.

c. A mixture of bigger and smaller denominations should be brought to meet various circumstances. For everyday costs and smaller vendors, think about packing between 50 and 100 AZN (about 30 to 60 USD) in smaller notes, and have some larger bills or extra cash on hand for bigger purchases or emergencies.

d. Safety: Use a money belt or a lockable wallet to keep your cash safe. To lessen the chance of theft, be aware of your surroundings and avoid flashing big sums of cash in public.

While having cash on hand might be useful, it's also a good idea to have a backup plan, such as a credit or debit card, as well as some emergency contact numbers for your bank, in case of any problems or unanticipated events.

Where to Find an Exchanger

There are various choices accessible to you if you need to convert money while you're in Baku, the capital of Azerbaijan. The locations in Baku where you may exchange money are listed in detail below:

Banks: The most dependable and safe locations to exchange money are banks. In Baku, several large banks provide currency exchange services. Search for reputable financial institutions like the International Bank of Azerbaijan, Kapital Bank, Bank of Baku, or PASHA Bank. These banks have locations all across the city, including in well-known locales like the city center and close to tourist attractions. Bank exchange rates are often competitive, and the transaction is secure and open.

Currency Exchange Offices: Baku is home to a large number of currency exchange offices. These offices often have signage outside that read "Exchange" or "Money Exchange." Particularly in crowded locations like Fountain Square, Nizami Street, and the Old City, they are not difficult to locate (Icherisheher). However, it's crucial to use these services with care since certain exchange offices could have unfair rates or additional costs. It's a good idea to examine rates at several exchange offices before choosing one.

Hotels: Many hotels in Baku provide their visitors with currency exchange facilities. But be aware that hotel rates may not be as affordable as those at banks or specialist currency bureaus. To make an educated choice, it is advised to enquire ahead about the exchange rates and charges.

Airports: Heydar Aliyev International Airport offers small-dollar currency exchange services for travelers that want instant cash upon arrival. In the arrivals and departures sections, there are currency exchange counters. However, keep in mind that exchange rates at airports are often worse than those in the city core. Consider converting just enough money to meet your immediate requirements, and then shop around for a better rate.

Automated Teller Machines (ATMs): In Baku, there are several ATMs that you may use to withdraw local money with your debit or credit card. However, it's crucial to confirm with your bank in advance if there are any limits or costs associated with foreign withdrawals. Finding ATMs connected to large banks is advised for greater withdrawal limits and better exchange rates since certain ATMs may have lower withdrawal limitations.

Keep your passport close by while exchanging currency in Baku since it can be needed for identification. To make sure you get the most for your money, it's also a good idea to evaluate exchange rates and costs across various providers.

Consider Travel Insurance

Travel insurance offers financial security and peace of mind in the event of unforeseen circumstances or crises that can arise while you are there. When visiting Baku, you should think about purchasing travel insurance for the following reasons:

Medical Emergencies: Travel insurance usually pays for medical costs, such as prescription drugs, hospital stays, and emergency medical evacuation. Having travel insurance assures that, in the case of a sickness or accident during your vacation, you will obtain essential medical treatment without having to pay astronomical costs.

Vacation Cancellation or Interruption: Because life is unpredictable, there may be instances when you must cancel or shorten your vacation. If you need to cancel or cut short your vacation due to a covered cause, such as sickness, accident, or family crises, travel insurance may pay you for planning, and non-refundable costs like flights, lodging, and excursions.

Baggage disasters may be highly stressful and annoying, such as lost or delayed luggage. When your baggage is lost, stolen, or damaged, travel insurance gives coverage, paying you to replace any necessary things and lessen the effect on your trip. Additionally, travel insurance may pay you back for the cost of purchasing essentials like clothes and toiletries if your luggage is delayed for a certain amount of time.

Travel Delays: Flight cancellations and delays are frequent, and they may ruin your plans and cost you more money. If you are significantly delayed for a covered cause, such as bad weather, mechanical problems, or strikes, travel insurance may pay for your meals, lodging, and transportation costs.

Personal Liability: Mishaps may occur when traveling, and if you inadvertently harm someone or destroy property, you might be held accountable. Personal liability coverage, which is sometimes included in travel insurance, may aid in defraying court costs or settlements if you are held accountable for such situations.

Emergency support Services: Many travel insurance plans include access to a hotline where you may call for support and guidance in case of crises. These services are often available around-the-clock. When you require aid with language translation, medical referrals, or organizing an emergency medical evacuation when traveling to a foreign nation, this may be very helpful.

Review the policy details, including coverage limitations, exclusions, and any unique requirements or restrictions, before acquiring travel insurance for your trip to Baku. Make sure the policy satisfies your requirements and corresponds with the activities you want to do while visiting.

Although it is not legally necessary to have travel insurance to visit Baku, it is highly recommended to guard against unforeseen circumstances and possible financial losses. It offers a safety net, enabling you to take pleasure in your journey in the knowledge that you are protected in the event of crises or unanticipated occurrences.

Medical Care Services

Modern hospitals, clinics, and specialized medical centers with cutting-edge equipment are now available in the city, which has seen substantial expansion in the healthcare sector in recent years. The medical services offered in Baku are described in detail below:

Hospitals: Baku is home to several reputed medical facilities that provide all-encompassing treatment. These hospitals include departments with expertise in a range of disciplines, including orthopedics, cancer, pediatrics, cardiology, and more. The Azerbaijan Medical University Hospital, Oil Workers Hospital, Central Clinic Hospital, and Baku Clinical Medical Center are a few of the city's well-known hospitals.

Specialized Medical Centers: Baku is home to a large number of hospitals that specialize in certain medical fields. These facilities provide cutting-edge therapies and services, sometimes in association with institutions from outside. The National Oncology Center, Cardiology Center, Neurology Center, and Baku Eye Clinic are a few important specialty facilities in Baku.

Emergency Care: Major hospitals in Baku have well-equipped emergency rooms that are open around the clock to provide prompt medical assistance. These divisions are manned with highly skilled medical personnel and furnished with cutting-edge life-saving tools. Residents and tourists may rely on these emergency care services to provide timely and effective treatment in the event of medical emergencies, such as accidents or severe illnesses.

Outpatient Clinics: There is a sizable network of outpatient clinics in Baku that provide general medical treatment, preventative care, and specialist consultations.

These clinics provide general check-ups, vaccines, diagnostic testing, and minor operations, among other services that address a variety of medical requirements. A lot of clinics in Baku are easily accessible and provide patients with flexible appointment times.

Diagnostic and imaging facilities: Baku is home to cutting-edge diagnostic and imaging facilities that provide a precise and prompt diagnosis. These institutions include MRI and CT scanners, ultrasound devices, and X-ray facilities, among other cutting-edge medical imaging equipment. Experienced radiologists and technicians guarantee the findings' proper interpretation, assisting in the process of making a diagnosis and formulating a treatment plan.

Rehabilitation Facilities: Baku is home to some facilities dedicated to recovering and enhancing patients' cognitive and physical abilities. For those suffering from operations, injuries, or chronic diseases, these facilities provide thorough rehabilitation programs. To help patients recover and live better lives, they provide treatments including physiotherapy, occupational therapy, speech therapy, and psychological assistance.

Dental Clinics: Dental care is a crucial component of health care, and Baku has a large selection of dental clinics with up-to-date technology and qualified dentists working in them. These dental offices provide a wide variety of dental services, such as regular checkups, oral hygiene regimens, restorative procedures, orthodontics, and oral surgery.

Pharmacy: Baku has a large number of pharmacies dispersed all around the city, enabling simple access to medicines and healthcare supplies. Many pharmacies are open twenty-four hours a day and sell prescription medicines, over-the-counter medicines, and a range of healthcare supplies. Pharmacists are ready to answer questions about drugs and provide instructions on how to use them properly.

Baku offers a wide variety of medical services to meet the various healthcare requirements of its citizens and tourists. The city offers access to top-notch healthcare services thanks to its contemporary hospitals, specialty medical centers, emergency care facilities, outpatient clinics, diagnostic centers, rehabilitation centers, dental clinics, and pharmacies. Baku is a center for healthcare in Azerbaijan due to the availability of experienced medical personnel, cutting-edge technology, and a dedication to enhancing healthcare.

Health Tips for Travelers

It's crucial to put your health and well-being first when traveling to Baku as a tourist. To help you stay healthy while on your visit, consider the following advice:

Drink plenty of water: Baku has warm temperatures, especially in the summer. To keep hydrated and prevent dehydration, it's important to drink lots of water throughout the day. If you're out exploring or doing strenuous activity, have a reusable water bottle with you and refill it periodically.

Azerbaijan gets a lot of sunlight, thus it's necessary to protect oneself from the sun's dangerous UV rays. To protect your skin and eyes from the sun, put on a hat with a broad brim, sunglasses, and sunscreen with a high SPF. To prevent sunburn and heat exhaustion during the warmest hours of the day, seek shade.

Be Wary of Food and Water: Although there are usually safe and sanitary food alternatives available in Baku, it is still advised to use care, especially when tasting street cuisine or dining at local restaurants. Eat only food that has been fully cooked and is served hot to lower your chance of contracting a foodborne disease. To avoid any possible gastrointestinal problems, stay away from drinking tap water and use bottled water instead.

Maintain appropriate hand hygiene during your vacation by practicing it. Regularly wash your hands with soap and water, particularly before eating or just after visiting the restroom in a public place. Use hand sanitizer with at least 60% alcohol if soap and water are not available.

Stay Active: It's crucial to include physical exercise in your daily routine even while you're on vacation. Baku has several chances for outdoor pursuits including cycling, hiking, and walking trips. Regular exercise not only keeps you in shape but also increases your energy and improves your general well-being.

Bring Enough Prescription Drugs: If you need to take any prescription drugs, be sure you pack enough of them. Carrying a modest first aid kit with basic supplies like painkillers, bandages, and antiseptic cream is also a smart idea. Learn the names of your drugs under their generic names in case you need to buy them locally.

Get Enough Sleep: Traveling may be exhausting, so prioritize rest and get enough sleep while you're away. You'll be able to keep up a healthy immune system and fully take pleasure in your hobbies if you do this. Choose a comfortable place to stay that meets your requirements, and create a regular sleep schedule.

Travel safely by taking the essential procedures to protect your security and welfare. Keep an eye on your surroundings, particularly in busy places, and safeguard your possessions. If you want to go outside of the city, choose safe modes of transportation and do your homework on trustworthy tour companies.

Prepare Yourself for Local Healthcare: Before your journey, do some research and make a note of the addresses and contact information of local hospitals and medical facilities in case of an emergency. Additionally, it's a good idea to obtain travel insurance that includes medical coverage in case you need treatment while away.

Respect the COVID-19 rules: Because the COVID-19 pandemic may still be present, it's important to be aware of the limits and criteria that apply in Baku. Adhere to the advised safety precautions, such as using masks while in public, exercising physical distance, and often hand sanitizing.

Remember that these suggestions are just basic advice; it is always advisable to speak with a medical expert or your travel doctor before leaving on your trip to Baku to get individualized guidance based on your unique medical requirements.

LQBTQ+Acceptance

In recent years, acceptance of LGBTQ+ people has advanced significantly in Baku. There is a rising push in the city towards more inclusion, visibility, and acceptance of the LGBTQ+ population, even if obstacles and biases persist.

The establishment of LGBTQ+ advocacy organizations and support groups is one of the noteworthy achievements in Baku's acceptance of LGBTQ+ people. These groups put in many hours to advance LGBTQ+ rights, increase knowledge of LGBTQ+ problems, and provide the community with a haven. To promote a feeling of belonging and solidarity among LGBTQ+

people and their supporters, they arrange events, seminars, and social gatherings.

Azerbaijan does not officially safeguard individuals' legal rights against discrimination based on their sexual orientation or gender identity, nor does it recognize same-sex marriages. However, things are progressively getting better. LGBTQ+ activists are actively pushing for legislative changes and broader acceptance of LGBTQ+ rights in Baku.

The LGBTQ+ community is becoming more well-recognized in Baku. Pride parades and other open celebrations of LGBTQ+ identities have gained popularity, despite certain restrictions and difficulties. These gatherings provide a venue for LGBTQ+ people and supporters to interact, express themselves, and fight for their rights.

The social environment in Baku has changed to welcome LGBTQ+ people. There are now more LGBTQ+-friendly pubs, clubs, and cafés than ever before, even if there may not be as many LGBTQ+-specific events and locations as in some other big cities. These businesses strive to provide welcoming environments where people may feel at home and express themselves freely.

Positive changes in the media environment have also been made concerning LGBTQ+ representation in Baku. Some media sources have begun discussing LGBTQ+ topics and publishing articles that highlight the perspectives of LGBTQ+ people. This greater exposure helps in dispelling prejudices and promoting an open discourse among members of society.

It's vital to remember that accepting LGBTQ+ people in Baku is not without its difficulties. Conservative ideas and ingrained cultural and social standards may still lead to stigma and prejudice. LGBTQ+ people may experience bullying, exclusion, and even violence in certain circumstances. However, the development over the last several years shows a greater understanding and readiness to deal with these problems.

Overall, Baku has seen improvements in LGBTQ+ acceptance, even if there is still work to be done. A culture that is moving toward more tolerance and acceptance of the LGBTQ+ population may be seen in the formation of advocacy groups, increasing exposure, and rising support from allies.

Emergency Contacts

In the event of an emergency or urgent situation, residents and tourists in Baku, the capital city of Azerbaijan, must have access to emergency contacts. For quick help and assistance, having access to accurate and trustworthy emergency contact information is crucial. The following is a comprehensive list of Baku's emergency contacts:

Services for Emergencies:
Police: In case of an emergency, dial 102 for Baku police. It needs to be used in instances of crimes, mishaps, or any other circumstance requiring police assistance.

Fire Department: Dial 101 to contact the Baku Fire Department in the case of a fire or any other emergency involving fire. They can manage rescue and firefighting operations thanks to their equipment.

To contact the Baku Ambulance Service in case of an emergency or for urgent medical help, dial 103. They provide both emergency medical services and hospital transportation.

Emergency & Crisis Centers:

State Crisis Management Center: Managing and organizing emergency response efforts are the responsibilities of the State Crisis Management Center in Baku. Contact information for them is +994 12 498 08 08.

State Marine Rescue Coordination Center: Dial +994 12 498 70 76 to reach the State Maritime Rescue Coordination Center if you need marine rescue or assistance whether on land or at water.

Medical Centers and Hospitals:

Baku Central Hospital is a significant healthcare institution that offers a broad variety of medical services. It is situated in the heart of the city. You may call their emergency room at +994 12 498 19 19.

City Clinical Hospital No. 1 is a well-known medical center in Baku and is located in the Nasimi neighborhood. The number to call to reach them and request emergency help is +994 12 492 26 36.

Consulates and Embassies:

Foreign Consulates: Baku is host to many foreign consulates and embassies. It is advised to have your country's embassy's contact information close at hand in case you need help or information as a foreign citizen. On the website of the Azerbaijani Ministry of Foreign Affairs, you may find a full list of foreign embassies and consulates in Baku.

Driving Assistance:

Roadside accidents or emergencies may be reported to the Baku Traffic Police by dialing 102. They can help and plan the essential steps.

Roadside assistance and car towing are provided by some private towing firms in Baku. In case of breakdowns or accidents, it is recommended to have the phone number of a dependable towing service handy.

It is crucial to keep in mind that emergency contact information may change over time, thus it is advised to double-check the most recent information with local or governmental authorities. Additionally, for a safer trip, educate yourself ahead with the local emergency contact numbers and services whether you're visiting Baku or any other foreign city.

Laws

To guarantee a secure and pleasurable journey, visitors to Baku must get acquainted with the local laws and ordinances. When visiting Baku, visitors should be aware of the following laws:

Visa Requirements: Tourists should research the visa requirements for their country of residence before going to Baku. To enter Azerbaijan, visitors from many nations must have a visa, which must be obtained in advance. The majority of nations may apply for visas online thanks to the e-visa system.

Passport and Identification: While visiting Baku, visitors must always have their passport with them or a duplicate of it. In case of crises, it's also a good idea to have a duplicate of any other crucial identifying papers, such as a driver's license or national ID card.

Drug Laws: Drug trafficking and possession are strictly prohibited in Azerbaijan. Possession, use, and trafficking of any kind of illegal narcotics, including marijuana, are prohibited. Violators risk harsh punishments, including incarceration.

Even though Baku has many beautiful vistas, it's vital to be aware of the photography regulations. Airports, some military and governmental structures, and other sensitive locations may not allow photography. Before shooting pictures in possibly off-limits locations, it's a good idea to get permission or check with the local authorities.

Azerbaijan is a nation with a large Muslim population, thus visitors should be considerate of the local traditions and customs. It is advised to avoid public shows of love and to dress modestly, especially while visiting sacred locations.

Alcohol Consumption: In Azerbaijan, the legal drinking age is 18. Although consuming alcohol is largely permitted in Baku, excessive drinking in public areas and public drunkenness are not encouraged and may result in penalties or even imprisonment.

The Azerbaijani Manat (AZN) is the country of Azerbaijan's official currency. Keep receipts for all transactions and only exchange money at approved banks or exchange bureaus. Declare any big quantities of money upon arrival or departure since it is prohibited to leave the nation with more cash than a specific amount.

Traffic rules: It's important to be knowledgeable of the regional traffic laws if you want to drive in Baku. All passengers in a car are required to wear seatbelts, and it is legally forbidden to drive when intoxicated. To avoid fees or penalties, it's also essential to adhere to speed limits, traffic signals, and parking restrictions.

Respect for Public Spaces and Monuments: Baku is renowned for its stunning architecture and ancient landmarks. It's crucial to respect these locations by avoiding damaging, polluting, or vandalizing public areas. For Baku's beauty to continue, environmental protection and cultural preservation are essential.

Tourists should use normal safety measures when visiting Baku, just like they would in any other city. Be watchful about your possessions, especially in busy places, and keep expensive goods hidden. Use trustworthy transportation, and pay attention to your surroundings, particularly at night.

Keep in mind that this is just a broad summary of the key legislation that affects visitors in Baku. When traveling to any foreign nation, it is always advisable to check with official government sources, ask for guidance from local officials, or check with your embassy to make sure you have the most recent information possible about laws and regulations.

Chapter 7: Planning and Financial Management

A well-thought-out strategy and wise money management are crucial for a hassle-free and pleasurable vacation. Here is a thorough explanation of planning advice and money-management suggestions for your trip to Baku.

· **Research and planning an itinerary:**

Before your journey, do an extensive study about Baku's tourist destinations, cultural activities, regional traditions, and travel needs.

Establish the length of your trip and make a thorough schedule that includes the must-see locations, the activities you want to do, and any special events you want to attend.

Prioritize your choices and schedule your time appropriately, taking into account the different attractions' and activities' running hours.

Documents for Travel and Insurance:

Make sure your passport is valid for at least six months after the day you want to travel.

To enter Azerbaijan, find out whether you need a visa and apply well in advance, if necessary.

Think about getting travel insurance that includes coverage for unexpected medical expenses, trip cancellations, and lost or stolen personal property.

Creating a budget and foreign exchange:

Establish your trip budget, taking into account lodging, transit, food, sights, shopping, and any other costs you foresee.

Learn about the Azerbaijani Manat (AZN), the native currency, and the current exchange rates.

Carry a variety of payment methods to ensure they are accepted extensively in Baku, including cash, credit cards, and debit card.

Transportation and lodging:

Pre-book your lodging while taking budget, location, and amenity considerations into account.

Look at the numerous modes of transportation in Baku, including public transit, taxis, and rental automobiles. Choose the method that best meets your demands and budget.

Eating and Dining:

Discover Baku's food, which is renowned for its unique tastes and culinary traditions.

Investigate well-known eateries and choices for street food, taking into account opinions and suggestions from residents and other tourists.

Set aside money for eating out, but also think about exploring your neighborhood's markets and supermarkets for less expensive meal alternatives.

Entertainment and Attractions:

Make a list of the major sights in Baku that you want to see.

Identify whether attractions or activities need reservations or entrance fees.

Look for tickets with discounts, bundles, or city passes that provide admission to many attractions at a lower cost.

Security and Safety:

Learn the local regulations, traditions, and emergency phone numbers in Baku.

Use hotel safes or take your items securely with you to ensure the protection of your property.

Before and during your journey, be aware of any travel advice or warnings published by Azerbaijan.

Monitoring Expenses:

Throughout your vacation, keep a record of your expenditures to check your budget and prevent going overboard.

Use a smartphone app or a pocket notepad to keep track of your spending on things like lodging, food, travel, attractions, and shopping.

Connectivity and Communication:

For information on foreign roaming arrangements, check with your cell service provider, or think about getting a local SIM card.

To remain connected without paying extra, look out for free Wi-Fi sites in Baku's hotels, cafés, and open spaces.

Emergency Resources:

In case of unanticipated events or unplanned costs during your vacation, set aside emergency money.

Carry a second credit card or put it in a safe digital wallet so you may access more money if necessary.

You can maximize your vacation while keeping within your budget by meticulously organizing your trip to Baku and managing your money.

The Need for Managing Finances when Traveling

When traveling, good money management is essential, and Baku, the capital of Azerbaijan, is no exception. Baku provides a dynamic fusion of contemporary attractions, historical landmarks, and a wide variety of cultural activities. It is crucial to practice solid money management if you want to make the most of your trip and prevent any unwarranted financial hardship. The following is a thorough explanation of why money management is crucial while visiting Baku:

Budgeting: Setting up a budget is the first step in effective money management. Baku has a lot to do, from seeing historical sites to dining on regional cuisine and shopping. You may organize your costs correctly and allocate money to necessary needs while still leaving money for pleasurable activities by creating a realistic budget.

Cost of Living: To effectively manage your money, you must be aware of the cost of living in Baku. Although there are both affordable and upscale accommodations available in the city, understanding the typical costs for lodging, food, transportation, and attractions can help you plan and stay within your budget.

The Azerbaijani Manat (AZN) is the currency used in Baku. You may maximize your financial investment by being knowledgeable about currency rates and selecting the most advantageous solutions. To prevent unfavorable exchange rates or fake currency, it is advised to exchange money at reputable banks or exchange offices rather than at hotels or unlicensed merchants.

Payment Options: Credit/debit cards are commonly accepted in most places in Baku, a modern city with a sophisticated financial infrastructure. Carrying some cash is still advised for smaller businesses, markets, and local transportation. You may make the necessary preparations and ensure that you have the funds to make the required payments by being aware of the accepted payment options.

Safety and Security: During your stay in Baku, financial management is crucial in maintaining your safety and security. It's crucial to keep your cash and valuables safe, and you should avoid flashing big sums of cash in public. You may protect your financial assets by utilizing secure ATMs, making copies of crucial papers, and using hotel safes.

Despite your best efforts to budget, unexpected costs may still occur during your vacation. It can be an unforeseen event, a health crisis, or a transportation problem. You may manage such crises without placing excessive pressure on your finances by having an emergency fund or contingency plan in place.

Local Customs and Tipping: Financial management in Baku requires an understanding of regional customs and tipping traditions. It is normal to give a little tip at restaurants, hotels, and other places where services are provided even when it is not required. Knowing these conventions can help you plan your gratuity budget and prevent any awkward situations or misunderstandings.

Shopping for souvenirs: Baku is renowned for its distinctive carpets, crafts, and traditional mementos. To prevent overspending, it is essential to set a budget and prioritize your purchases. Making educated decisions and obtaining the most value for your money may be accomplished by comparing costs, haggling in marketplaces, and asking locals for advice.

Travel insurance: Good financial management also involves safeguarding yourself from unanticipated events. When visiting Baku, you must have travel insurance since it may cover unexpected costs such as lost luggage, flight cancellations, and medical crises. The peace of mind that comes from having complete travel insurance helps shield you from any financial damages.

To have a stress-free and pleasurable trip to Baku, efficient money management is essential. You can control your spending and make the most of your vacation by setting up a budget, learning about the cost of living, keeping an eye on foreign exchange rates, and choosing your payment options wisely. A safe and financially healthy trip will also benefit from having travel insurance, being ready for unforeseen costs, and following local traditions.

Savings Tips for Travelers

Some cost-cutting suggestions might help you maximize your vacation without going over budget. Here are some thorough ideas for conserving money while having fun in Baku:

Accommodation:

Instead of staying in a fancy hotel, think about staying in a guesthouse, a hostel, or a budget hotel. At a fraction of the price, these alternatives often provide cozy, spotless accommodations.

When making a reservation for lodging, search online for discounts and specials. Several travel websites provide discounted prices or unique packages that may help you save money.

Transportation:

Use the metro, buses, and trams as well as other forms of public transit to navigate the city. Public transportation in Baku is effective and reasonably priced, and it serves the most popular tourist destinations.

Only use taxis when required. Taxi charges may add up rapidly, so wherever feasible, choose public transit.

To get about the city, think about walking or renting a bike. The city core of Baku is small and includes a lot of attractions that are close to one another.

Dining:

Rather than eating at tourist-oriented restaurants and cafés, eat at local eateries. Local restaurants often provide affordable genuine and delectable Azerbaijani food.

Look for specific lunch menus or lunch specials that are available at a discount at certain times. This may be an excellent opportunity to sample regional cuisine without spending a fortune.

Think about doing part of your cooking. You may shop for food at nearby markets or supermarkets and make your meals if your lodging has a kitchen.

Activities and Sightseeing:

Take advantage of places and activities that are free or inexpensive. There are several public parks, gardens, and other locations in Baku that are open to the public and provide lovely city views.

To take advantage of any cheap admission prices or special deals, do your research and organize your touring ahead of time. Depending on the day of the week or the time of day, several attractions may offer reduced pricing.

Consider getting a Baku Card, which provides savings on a number of the city's attractions, museums, and transit options.

Shopping:

Investigate regional markets and bazaars for genuine souvenirs, spices, and traditional goods that are cheaply priced. To obtain the greatest pricing, haggle and bargain.

Avoid shopping in upscale malls and shops because the cost might be much greater than in local marketplaces.

whether you want to buy bigger products or pricey souvenirs, think about seeing whether you can get a VAT refund at the airport. You may be able to reduce your buying costs as a result.

Change of Currencies:

When exchanging money, use caution. To guarantee you get a fair exchange rate without additional costs or exorbitant charges, use renowned exchange offices or ATMs to withdraw cash.

Before completing a purchase, compare the currency rates and costs at several locations. Certain exchange offices may have better rates than others.

Security and Safety:

Take the required procedures to protect your possessions to prevent any unforeseen costs. Be on the lookout for pickpockets and safeguard your belongings.

Carry your cash and cards in a safe wallet or money belt. Keep a duplicate of your passport and other critical papers in case they are lost or stolen, and try to avoid carrying significant amounts of cash.

You may enjoy your trip to Baku while keeping your spending under control by using this money-saving advice. Plan, look into your alternatives, and make use of the city's reasonably priced public transit system and inexpensive attractions.

Tips for Bargaining and Negotiating

It's important to be prepared and aware of regional norms while haggling and negotiating in Baku, whether you're looking for souvenirs, visiting local bazaars, or doing business. Here are some pointers to assist you in negotiating and bargaining in Baku:

Before entering into discussions or negotiating, familiarize yourself with the local norms and culture. Maintaining a nice and polite demeanor will go a long way since Azerbaijanis value manners and respect.

Conduct rigorous market research before visiting Baku's marketplaces or starting a business negotiation to understand what the going rate is for the goods or services you are interested in. You can bargain more skillfully and with more reasonable expectations if you have this information.

Begin with a grin and a polite hello to start your bargaining or negotiating session. Successful negotiations may take place in an atmosphere that is promoted by developing a good rapport and connection with the other side.

Take Your Time: Negotiating in Baku is a deliberate and lengthy procedure. Instead of rushing into a decision, take your time to consider all of your alternatives and compare pricing. With this strategy, you can survey the market, gauge the quality, and bargain for better conditions.

Haggling is a regular occurrence in the marketplaces of Baku, but it's necessary to do it politely. Begin by making a smaller offer than you're prepared to make, and then haggle with the seller to get to an agreement. Throughout the procedure, keep your composure while being courteous.

Know When to Walk Away: Be ready to leave if you are unable to come to an amicable arrangement if the seller's asking price is too high. A readiness to depart might sometimes cause the other party to reevaluate their offer and perhaps come back with a better one.

Think About Bulk Purchases: If you're interested in making many purchases, think about doing it in bulk. In

Baku, many vendors are more willing to provide discounts when they can sell more merchandise. You may be able to save money and improve your negotiating position by negotiating a bulk price.

Even though several Baku residents speak English, it might be helpful to acquire a few basic Azerbaijani words while haggling and negotiating. You may interact with the locals more easily and manage the process by using basic greetings, numbers, and words about costs and negotiations.

Use Local Contacts: If at all feasible, enlist the aid of a local contact who can support you during negotiating or talks, such as a guide or a reliable acquaintance. Their familiarity with the area and language abilities may be quite helpful in guaranteeing clear communication and getting the best bargain.

have Calm and Be Respectful: When bargaining or negotiating in Baku, it's important to be patient and have a cool head. You can have a harder time getting what you want if you act angry or hostile. Instead of seeing the process as a power struggle, treat it as a cordial dialogue.

Never forget that reaching a win-win deal is the aim of bargaining and negotiating in Baku. You may increase your chances of having fruitful discussions and pleasurable buying experiences in this wonderful city by heeding these suggestions and respecting local norms.

Tax-Free Shopping and Refund

A method called "tax-free shopping and refund" enables international tourists to make purchases in another nation and be reimbursed for the value-added tax (VAT) they spent on such transactions. By offering an incentive for tourists to spend money when traveling to a certain location, this system aims to promote tourism and strengthen the economy.

In Baku, the capital of Azerbaijan, visitors who meet the requirements may shop tax-free and get refunds. Here is a thorough explanation of how it operates:

Eligibility: You must fulfill several requirements to be eligible for tax-free shopping in Baku. This usually entails being a non-Azerbaijani resident with a temporary visiting status, such as a tourist or business traveler. Before making any purchases, it is crucial to confirm the nation's unique needs and laws.

Look for stores with tax-free shopping badge or sign to identify participating retailers. These businesses engage in the tax return program as merchants. High-end malls, boutiques, and duty-free stores, which are well-known shopping destinations in Baku, often provide tax-free shopping options. Remember that not all retailers take part, so it's best to find out before.

Making Purchases: Be sure to let the salesperson know that you want to take advantage of tax-free shopping when you make a purchase. They'll provide you with the required documentation and walk you through the procedure. You must save your receipts since you will need them to subsequently get a VAT refund.

VAT Refund Forms: The salesperson will provide you with a tax refund form, sometimes referred to as a Tax-Free Shopping Cheque or a Global Blue Cheque, that contains information about your purchase, the amount of VAT you paid, and the store's data. As you fill out the form, be careful to be as precise as possible.

Validation at Customs: You must go through customs before leaving Baku. Present the customs officer with your goods, receipts, and completed tax refund papers for verification. The papers will be examined and stamped as export documentation.

Refund Options: There are a few ways to have your VAT refunded in Baku. Receiving a cash refund at the airport is the most typical procedure. You may show your stamped documents at designated tax refund desks or kiosks at certain airports to get an instant cash refund or have the money refunded to your credit card. Alternatively, you may choose to get the refund through electronic transfer or credit card, based on the choices offered.

There is often a minimum purchase requirement to be eligible for a tax refund. Depending on the nation and the kind of products bought, this sum could change. To make sure your purchases comply with the criteria for tax-free shopping in Baku, it is important to examine the relevant rules.

Time Limit for Refund Request: After the date of purchase, you typically have a certain amount of time to request a VAT refund. It's important to be informed of the exact regulations since this time frame might change. It may not be feasible to request a refund after you have left Azerbaijan, so be sure to finish the refund procedure before doing so.

It's important to keep in mind that tax-free shopping and refund procedures might differ from one nation to the next and that precise rules may alter over time. To guarantee a simple and hassle-free experience, it is always advised to verify the most recent information and instructions issued by the authorities or to speak with the store or tax refund service provider in Baku.

Top Markets

A bustling and multicultural city, Baku provides a variety of marketplaces where residents and visitors may enjoy the customs, food, and culture of the region. The following are a few of Baku's best markets:

One of the biggest and most well-known marketplaces in Baku is Taza Bazaar (Bazar), which is situated in the city's center. There are several fresh fruits, veggies, spices, meats, and dairy products available in this crowded market. It is a must-visit location for food lovers because of the living environment and the chance to connect with local sellers.

The çrişhr (Old City) Market, which is located within the Old City's medieval walls, provides a classic shopping experience with its modest stores and winding lanes. You may discover a wide variety of goods here, such as carpets, antiques, regional crafts, spices, local delicacies, and mementos. It's a wonderful location to fully experience Azerbaijan's rich cultural history.

Nizami Street (Torgovaya): One of Baku's busiest and liveliest retail districts is Nizami Street. It is a haven for fashion fans and shopaholics since it is bordered by a ton of boutiques, big brands, and luxury stores. A variety of apparel, accessories, jewelry, cosmetics, and gadgets are available here. The street's bustling ambiance is enhanced by the presence of cafés, restaurants, and entertainment places.

The Nasimi neighborhood's Yashil Bazaar (Green Market) is well-known for its fresh food, which includes fruits, vegetables, herbs, and spices. It provides a wonderful chance to sample regional delicacies and purchase organic and locally produced goods.

Additionally, there are vendors at the market that offer honey, dried fruits, nuts, and traditional Azerbaijani delicacies.

Park Bulvar Shopping Mall is a prominent location in Baku if you desire a contemporary shopping experience. The Caspian Sea beachfront is home to this shopping center, which also has a multiplex theater, a food court with a variety of eating choices, and a play area for kids. It's the ideal location for relaxing, shopping, and taking in the breathtaking sea views.

The Binagadi district's Sharg Bazari (Eastern Bazaar) is a bustling market with a focus on apparel, accessories, home goods, and electronics. Locals seeking a broad variety of things at reasonable costs find it especially appealing. The market also has food stands and restaurants where visitors may sample traditional Azerbaijani cuisine.

Genclik Mall is one of Baku's biggest retail malls, and it is located close to the city's core. There are several national and international brands there, as well as a sizable supermarket, a theater district, a bowling alley, and an indoor amusement park. The mall is a favorite with families and consumers since it accommodates a variety of interests and preferences.

These are just a few examples of some of Baku's best marketplaces. Baku has plenty to offer everyone, whether they are searching for traditional items, regional food, high-end clothing, or a contemporary shopping experience. In addition to being a terrific place to buy, exploring these markets offers a chance to get to know the people and learn about the distinctive tastes and goods of Azerbaijan.

Chapter 8: Tourist Attractions and Fun Activities

Tourist Attractions

The following are a few of Baku's major tourist attractions:

The Old City, also known as Icherisheher, is Baku's historical core and a UNESCO World Heritage Site. With its tiny, twisting lanes adorned with historic structures like the famous Maiden Tower and the Palace of the Shirvanshahs, it is encircled by old walls. You may visit a variety of museums, art galleries, antique stores, and quaint cafés in the Old City.

Flame Towers: One of Baku's most recognizable contemporary monuments is the Flame Towers. These three towers have been constructed to mimic flames, and when they are lit up at night, the effect is breathtaking.

The Fairmont Baku Hotel, which offers expansive views of the city, is located in one of the towers.

Heydar Aliyev Center: The Heydar Aliyev Center is a marvel of architecture created by famous architect Zaha Hadid. This modern cultural facility hosts conferences, concerts, and exhibits. Its flowing and cutting-edge style has come to represent Baku's modernism.

The Baku Boulevard is a lovely waterfront promenade that spans along the Caspian Sea. It is located in the Seaside National Park. With its lush green parks, fountains, cafés, and restaurants, it provides a picturesque getaway from the bustle of the city. You may take a leisurely boat ride, walk along the promenade, or hire a bike.

The intriguing religious landmark is known as the Ateshgah Fire Temple is situated outside of Baku. Originally, Zoroastrians who revered the perpetual flame used it as a site of devotion. The temple has unusual pentagonal-shaped walls and a subterranean room with flames made of natural gas.

Gobustan National Park is a UNESCO World Heritage Site that is approximately an hour's drive from Baku. It is well-known for its ancient rock art and archaeological value. The area's rich history and culture may be discovered here, along with ancient rock sculptures and mud volcanoes.

Carpet Museum: The Carpet Museum is a must-see for people interested in textiles and handicrafts. Baku is known for its traditional carpet weaving. The museum showcases a sizable collection of Azerbaijani carpets, exhibiting its unique patterns and significance to the country's culture.

The Eurovision Song Contest was held at Baku Crystal Hall in 2012, and since then, it has been a well-liked location for musical performances and other events. It is a noteworthy architectural attraction due to its striking glass façade and modern design.

Gyz Galasy (Maiden Tower): The Maiden Tower is a historic building within the Old City that has come to represent Baku. The tower has a museum inside where you can learn about the city's past and folklore and enjoy expansive city views.

The National Museum of History of Azerbaijan offers a thorough picture of the country's past and present. Its vast collection of antiquities, which includes archaeological discoveries, traditional attire, weapons, and artwork, helps visitors get a better knowledge of the history of the nation.

These are only a handful of Baku's numerous tourist attractions. The city is a fascinating tourist destination because of its distinctive fusion of the ancient and the contemporary, as well as its thriving culture and welcoming people.

Educational Attractions and Museums

The city provides a variety of educational landmarks and museums that give visitors a look into its history and the chance to learn about its artistic, literary, and scientific accomplishments. The following is a thorough explanation of a few of Baku's top museums and educational attractions:

The Azerbaijan National Museum of History is a must-see destination for history buffs and is situated in the center of Baku. It presents a huge assortment of artifacts and exhibits that cover the history of the nation from prehistoric times to the present. Over 300,000 exhibits, including artwork, manuscripts, cultural artifacts, and archaeological discoveries, are kept at the museum. The many exhibits featuring ancient remains, medieval history, and Azerbaijan's rich cultural heritage are open to visitors.

Heydar Aliyev Center: Designed by famous architect Zaha Hadid, the Heydar Aliyev Center is a focal point for cultural and educational events in addition to being a work of art. It sponsors several exhibits, conferences, and seminars on a range of subjects, including history, technology, design, and art. Additionally, the center has multimedia exhibits and interactive displays that provide visitors with a unique educational experience.

Museum of Azerbaijani Literature: The Museum of Azerbaijani Literature honors the nation's literary legacy and is located in the center of Baku's historic district. It features the writings of notable Azerbaijani playwrights, poets, and authors throughout history. The museum's collection of manuscripts, rare books, authors' personal effects, and multimedia displays provide a thorough overview of Azerbaijani literature. Visitors may explore Azerbaijani literature to learn more about the nation's literary heritage.

Museum of Modern Art: The Museum of Modern Art is a thriving cultural center that exhibits the works of national and foreign artists. It was the first museum devoted to modern art in Azerbaijan. Paintings, sculptures, installations, and multimedia works are among the modern and contemporary art on display at the museum. To encourage people to interact with the art and investigate various creative forms, it also provides a variety of temporary exhibits, educational events, and workshops.

The Tofik Bakhramov Stadium is a fascinating educational attraction for football aficionados and other sports enthusiasts. In addition to serving as a location for football games, this historic stadium, which bears the name of the famous Azerbaijani football referee, also has a modest museum devoted to the history of football in Azerbaijan. The museum showcases artifacts, images, and hands-on exhibits that reflect the nation's football accomplishments and love for the game.

The Baku Museum of Miniature Books is a distinctive and intriguing educational attraction that is situated in the Old City. The museum has the distinction of being the only one in the world devoted exclusively to tiny books. A magnificent collection of more than 6,000 tiny books from many nations and eras may be found at the museum. Visitors may take in carefully made miniature books and discover the background of the publication of miniature books.

The Azerbaijan National Academy of Sciences is a prestigious organization devoted to advancing scientific knowledge and instruction. It provides numerous conferences, seminars, and instructional programs spanning a variety of scientific fields. The site of the academy is also home to several scientific museums, such as the Museum of Natural History, the Museum of Astronomy, and the Museum of Archaeology, where guests may discover the marvels of science and discover the contributions made by Azerbaijan to many academic disciplines.

Festivals and Events

Baku has a lot of festivals and events throughout the year that honor the arts, music, sports, and cultural heritage. Both residents and visitors are drawn to these celebrations because they give them a chance to take in the lively environment and discover the city's distinctive cultural attractions. The following list of notable festivals and events that take place in Baku is in-depth:

The Baku International Jazz Festival is an annual festival of jazz music from all over the globe that takes place in March. For a series of performances, seminars, and jam sessions, the festival gathers accomplished jazz performers and fans. It promotes cross-cultural understanding and respect for this musical genre by showcasing a wide variety of jazz genres and facilitating partnerships between foreign and local musicians.

The Baku International Film Festival, commonly referred to as "Baku IFF," is a significant occasion in the city's cultural calendar. The festival, which is held in

September, screens a broad range of movies, including dramas, comedies, documentaries, and shorts, to promote both Azerbaijani and foreign cinema. It gives performers, directors, and filmmakers a stage on which to present their work and involves the local public in insightful debates about cinema and its social implications.

The Baku Shopping Festival is a one-month-long spectacle of shopping that takes place every October. With discounts, promotions, and special deals at a variety of retail establishments, this festival provides residents and tourists with a distinctive shopping experience. Additionally, the event has fashion presentations, musical performances, cultural exhibits, and food vendors, bringing joy to the whole city.

Baku International Theater Festival: Baku is a significant center for the performing arts, and it organizes this festival every year. This festival, which takes place in November, features a broad selection of theatrical works from Azerbaijan and other countries. It includes performances in a range of genres, such as experimental theater, comedy, dance, and drama. Renowned theatrical companies and directors are drawn to the festival, which benefits the city's cultural life.

Novruz Bayram: The traditional Azerbaijani festival of Novruz Bayram is observed on the eve of the spring equinox, which usually occurs on March 20 or 21. During this festival, Baku comes alive with vivacious celebrations as people come together to welcome the start of spring. Outdoor games, traditional music and dance performances, public concerts, and traditional food preparation and sharing are all part of the celebrations. Baku's Novruz Bayram festivities provide a chance to get a personal look at the native way of life.

Baku Formula 1 Grand Prix: In April or May, Baku hosts the thrilling Baku Formula 1 Grand Prix, which is held on the city's streets. This well-known international race draws fans of racing from all around the globe. The city's famous attractions may be seen in exquisite detail as the race course travels through it. The Grand Prix includes many supporting events, concerts, and parties in addition to the main race, which energizes the entire city.

Baku International Jazz Festival: The Baku International Jazz Festival is another significant jazz event held in Baku. Internationally renowned jazz musicians and jazz fans come together for this October event. The festival offers a platform for musicians to demonstrate their abilities and collaborate musically through some concerts, jam sessions, and workshops. The Baku International Jazz Festival enhances the city's standing as a regional center for jazz music.

Enjoyable sports and activities

You can participate in the following popular sporting events while visiting Baku:

Football (soccer): Baku has a thriving soccer scene and several world-class stadiums. The Baku Olympic Stadium, which held the 2019 UEFA Europa League

Final, is the most notable. Depending on the season, you can watch thrilling local or even international matches. Football games in Baku have an electrifying atmosphere that makes them a must-try experience for sports fans.

Watersports: Baku, which is located on the Caspian Sea's coast, provides excellent opportunities for a variety of watersports. You can enjoy sports like windsurfing, parasailing, jet skiing, and wakeboarding. The coastline of Baku is home to some well-equipped water sports facilities that offer equipment rental and professional instruction to make sure that participants of all skill levels have a safe and enjoyable time.

Annually, Baku hosts the Formula 1 Grand Prix, which is held on an exhilarating street circuit in the middle of the city. The Azerbaijan Grand Prix provides an exceptional opportunity to see fast-paced motorsport action against Baku's stunning architecture. The event draws racing fans from around the world and provides an exhilarating experience for spectators.

Whether you prefer road cycling or mountain biking, Baku offers fantastic cycling opportunities. Cycling paths throughout the city's parks and along its seafront enable visitors to explore while taking in the stunning scenery. If you enjoy mountain biking, visit the nearby Gobustan National Park where you can find difficult trails surrounded by amazing rock formations.

Tennis: Baku offers both recreational and professional players well-maintained tennis courts and facilities. You can reserve sessions at exclusive clubs or rent public courts. Additionally, Baku hosts international tennis tournaments, attracting top-ranked players from around the world. If you're passionate about tennis, you may even find opportunities for training and coaching during your visit.

Martial Arts: Baku has a rich martial arts culture, and you can immerse yourself in various disciplines. Azerbaijani wrestling, known as "Koresh," is a traditional sport that showcases strength and technique. You can watch live matches or even take part in training sessions to learn the basics. Additionally, Baku offers martial arts gyms and dojos where you can practice disciplines like judo, taekwondo, and karate.

Golf: Golf enthusiasts can indulge in their favorite sport at the Dreamland Golf Club, located just outside Baku. This 18-hole championship course provides a picturesque setting, surrounded by beautiful countryside. The club offers top-notch facilities, including a driving range, putting greens, and professional coaching services. Whether you're a beginner or an experienced golfer, you can enjoy a relaxing day on the fairways.

Hiking and Trekking: Nature lovers can discover various options for hiking and trekking in the neighborhood of Baku. The adjacent Absheron Peninsula provides magnificent routes, where you may explore varied landscapes, including mountains, woods, and coastal locations. The famous trek to Yanardag (the "Burning Mountain") gives a unique experience as you observe natural gas burning continually on the surface.

Chapter 9: Day Trips and Excursions

Explore Wildlife and Nature

Baku, which is located on the Caspian Sea's coast, offers a unique chance to experience a range of habitats, from coastal regions to woods and mountains. Here is a thorough explanation of what to anticipate while visiting Baku's wildlife and natural environment.

Park National Gobustan:

Gobustan National Park, which is around 60 kilometers southwest of Baku, is a must-see location for nature lovers. The amazing rock formations, mud volcanoes, and historic petroglyphs of this UNESCO World Heritage Site are well known. Numerous plant and animal species, including gazelles, wild boars, wolves, and other bird species, call the park's rocky terrain home. The park may be explored for a chance to see the unadulterated beauty of Azerbaijan's landscapes and discover its long history.

Park national d'Absheron:

Another important natural landmark in the area is Absheron National Park, which is located on the Absheron Peninsula not far from Baku. This protected area is around 783 hectares in size and includes a variety of ecosystems, such as woods, semi-desert landscapes, and coastal wetlands. A sanctuary for a variety of migrating bird species, the park is a birdwatcher's heaven. Other animals, reptiles, and amphibians that live there include the Caspian seal, gazelles, foxes, and tortoises. Visitors may take advantage of escorted tours, birding excursions, and educational activities to learn more about the region's distinctive environment.

Caspian Sea:

Exploring the natural world on the sea is made possible by Baku's advantageous position on the Caspian Sea coast. The Caspian Sea is the world's largest enclosed inland body of water and is home to a diverse marine ecosystem. You could see different bird species while visiting the shoreline, including pelicans, cormorants, and gulls. You could even be fortunate enough to see dolphins or seals swimming in the ocean. Additionally, recreational fishing excursions are available for anglers, and some businesses provide boat cruises to discover the beauty of the sea and see marine life up close.

Park National Shahdag:

Northeast of Baku, in the Greater Caucasus Mountains, is a superb site for people looking for a mountainous adventure: Shahdag National Park. Over 130,000 hectares of this lovely park are available for a variety of outdoor activities. Visitors may embark on hikes through breathtaking alpine meadows in the summer, explore old-growth woods, and see animals like bears, wild goats, and eagles. Shahdag becomes a well-known ski resort in the winter, offering chances for snowboarding, skiing, and other winter sports.

(Burning Mountain) Yanardag:

Yanardag, popularly known as the Burning Mountain, is a unique experience that highlights Baku's natural beauty even if it is not strictly a wildlife location. A spectacular scene is produced by a natural gas fire that has been blazing for generations on the Absheron Peninsula. It seems as if the mountain is always on fire because of the several-meter-high flames that are fed by the subsurface gas reserves. Visitors will enjoy this natural occurrence and photographers will have a beautiful background to work with.

Baku offers fantastic chances to discover animals and the natural world in a range of settings, from national parks and mountains to the Caspian Sea shore.

Overview of a Solo Trip

Here is a thorough rundown of what a single trip to Baku may provide:

Accommodations: There are many places to stay in Baku, from opulent hotels to inexpensive hostels and welcoming guesthouses. Due to its historical importance and easy proximity to the city's main attractions, the city center, sometimes referred to as the Old City or Inner City (Icheri Sheher), is a well-liked place to stay.

The UNESCO-listed Old City, a fascinating tangle of winding alleyways, old structures, and monuments, is a great place to start your solo journey. The beautiful Palace of the Shirvanshahs, the recognizable Maiden Tower, and a plethora of quaint cafés, stores, and art galleries are all located inside its borders.

Modern Architecture: Baku is well known for its cutting-edge structures. The distinctive Flame Towers, a group of three buildings that dominate the city's skyline and are particularly stunning at night when lighted, should not be missed. Other notable structures include Baku Crystal Hall, which hosted the 2012 Eurovision Song Contest, and the Heydar Aliyev Center, which was created by famous architect Zaha Hadid.

Visit Baku's many museums and cultural institutes to fully experience the city's rich cultural history. The large collection on display at the Azerbaijan National Museum of History spans the whole of the nation's history, from prehistoric periods to the present. Art lovers might also pay a visit to the Azerbaijan Carpet Museum and the Museum of Modern Art.

Boulevard and Seaside Park: Enjoy a leisurely walk along the Boulevard, Baku's seafront boulevard. It boasts breathtaking views of the Caspian Sea, as well as parks, cafés, restaurants, and entertainment venues, and stretches for many kilometers. A must-see in Baku is the renowned Ferris wheel, the Carpet Museum, and the building that resembles a rolled-up carpet.

Gourmet Delights: With a wide variety of Azerbaijani and other cuisines, Baku is a gastronomic paradise. Enjoy traditional Azerbaijani fare including kebabs, plov (rice pilaf), and dolma (stuffed vegetables). Don't forget to taste the native tea and pakhlava and shekerbura pastries. Visit neighborhood eateries, food carts on the streets, and busy markets like Taza Bazaar to learn more about the city's diverse culinary culture.

Day visits: Day visits to local sights are made simple by Baku's advantageous position. Visit the Gobustan National Park, which is designated by UNESCO and is renowned for its ancient rock sculptures. Explore the historic Ateshgah Zoroastrian shrine or go to the Absheron Peninsula to see the stunning Yanar Dag (Burning Mountain) and the charming beach village of Qobustan.

Nightlife & entertainment: Baku has a thriving nightlife with a wide variety of pubs, clubs, and live music venues. Take in the city's nightlife, where you may party all night long or just unwind with a drink while admiring the breathtaking views from rooftop bars.

Safety and Hospitality: Baku is a safe and welcoming location for lone travelers due to its great hospitality and friendly residents. English is commonly spoken in tourist parts of the city, which makes it easier to communicate and find your way about. The city also boasts a developed infrastructure and dependable transit systems.

Is a Solo Trip Safe?

The colorful culture, extensive history, and breathtaking architecture of Baku are well-known. To protect your safety, it's crucial to follow specific guidelines while visiting any place. The following is a thorough explanation of safety precautions to take while traveling alone in Baku:

General Safety: Violent crimes are uncommon in Baku, which is seen to be a safe city for travelers. Being careful and aware of your surroundings is always a good idea, particularly in busy or touristy regions. Keep a watch on your stuff and be aware of pickpockets.

Accommodations: Pick trustworthy lodging alternatives like hotels or guesthouses in established neighborhoods. Read reviews, take into account location, and place an emphasis on security measures like 24-hour reception and strong locks. Additionally, it's a good idea to let the front desk or employees know if you're traveling alone and about any potential plans you may have while there.

Transportation: Taxis, public buses, and the metro are just a few of the alternatives available in Baku. In general, taxis are secure, but make sure you only use authorized taxi services and determine a fee before beginning the journey. Be watchful of your things while taking public transit, and stay away from congested places during rush hour.

Exploration: You may go alone to several of Baku's attractions. Popular tourist attractions worth seeing include the Heydar Aliyev Center, Maiden Tower, Flame Towers, and the Old City (Icherisheher). When going out at night, particularly, stay in crowded, well-lit locations. Avoiding secluded or dimly lit locations is also a good idea, especially if you are unfamiliar with the region.

Cultural Sensitivity: Honoring the traditions and practices of the destination is essential to having a secure and comfortable solo journey. The majority of the population in Azerbaijan is Muslim, thus it's vital to dress modestly, particularly while visiting places of worship or more conservative neighborhoods. Learn about the traditions of the area, and take care of how you behave and deal with people.

Although English is commonly used in tourist areas, hotels, and restaurants, Azerbaijani is the official language. However, learning a few fundamental Azerbaijani words might improve your relationships and make it simpler for you to get about the city.

Emergency Contacts: Before your journey, write down crucial phone numbers such as those for the local emergency services, your embassy, and your lodging. It's usually advantageous to have these specifics on hand in case of any unanticipated events.

Solo Activities: To improve your safety and make the most of your solo travel, think about signing up for planned tours or other guided activities. While delivering a group environment that assures you're not completely alone, these excursions may give insightful perspectives into the city's history and culture.

Socializing: There are several pubs, clubs, and restaurants in Baku's thriving nightlife scene. While it is normally safe to interact with others, use caution while meeting new people and limit your alcohol intake. It's wise to be mindful of your surroundings, inform someone of your intentions, and refrain from drinking excessively.

Local Tips: Talking to locals may provide you with insightful information about the place and its culture. On where to go, dine, and explore that is secure, they may advise. However, be wary of accepting offers from strangers, and follow your gut when you're in an unusual circumstance.

In conclusion, it's vital to take care and be alert of your surroundings even though Baku is typically regarded as safe for solitary travelers. You may have a safe and enjoyable solo trip to Baku by taking reasonable safety measures, following local traditions, and remaining informed.

Websites, Applications, and Resources that are Useful

There are many useful applications, websites, and other services that may improve your experience and help you get about the city. A thorough explanation of a few of these resources is provided below:

App for Baku Travel Guide: The app for Baku Travel Guide is a comprehensive mobile resource that offers in-depth details on the city's attractions, eateries, lodging alternatives, transit options, and more. It is a useful resource for learning about Baku since it provides interactive maps, audio tours, and user evaluations.

Website of Baku tourists: Baku Tourism's official website offers useful information about the city's historical sites, cultural activities, festivals, and tourist services. It gives you information about Baku's rich history, architecture, and regional cultures so you can successfully arrange your schedule.

Known for its user-generated ratings and suggestions, TripAdvisor is a well-known travel website and mobile application that provides information on hotels, restaurants, sights, and activities in Baku. Based on the experiences of other visitors, it may assist you in locating the top destinations to visit, eat at, and stay at.

Access to public transit, including buses, the metro, and the Baku Funicular, is made possible through the reloadable contactless card known as the BakuCard. The card provides reduced rates and may be acquired in some sites around the city. Additionally, it offers free entrance to several sights, making it an affordable choice for travelers.

The Baku City Circuit app is a need if you want to visit Baku for the Formula 1 Azerbaijan Grand Prix. It provides timetables, track information, real-time race updates, and interactive circuit maps. It improves your experience by giving you access to special material and making it possible for you to carefully follow the race.

The Baku Transport app offers details about Baku's public transportation system's timetables, tariffs, and routes. It has a travel planning tool that makes it easier to go about the city via bus, metro, tram, and funicular. Additionally, the app offers real-time data on bus and subway arrivals to keep you informed while traveling.

Websites offering restaurant suggestions, food tours, and insights into Azerbaijani cuisine are available on food guide platforms like "Baku Foodies" and "Baku Delights," which may be used to discover Baku's unique culinary scene. They can assist you in finding regional specialties, well-known eateries, and undiscovered treasures for an unforgettable dining experience.

Websites for Baku Museums: Baku is home to a large number of museums and cultural establishments that highlight the history, art, and legacy of the nation. Information about exhibits, hours of operation, admission costs, and special events may be found on the websites of attractions including the Heydar Aliyev Center, Azerbaijan Carpet Museum, and Azerbaijan National Museum of History. By checking these resources beforehand, you may schedule your museum visits appropriately.

Websites for Currency Exchange Rates: For the most recent information on currency exchange rates, check out XE.com or OANDA. To ensure you have the most up-to-date information when converting your money to the Azerbaijani Manat (AZN), these sites provide accurate and real-time exchange rates.

Apps that provide extensive maps of Baku, including sites of interest, driving directions, and offline accessibility, include Google Maps, and Maps. me, and HERE WeGo. With the aid of these applications, you may navigate a city, identify points of interest, and learn about local amenities like restaurants, ATMs, and pharmacies.

You may make the most of your trip to Baku by using these websites, applications, and services. You can discover the city's rich cultural history, sample regional specialties, and travel more effectively.

Conclusion

In conclusion, Baku is a dynamic and alluring place that provides a unique fusion of tradition, culture, and modernity. This travel guide has examined the city's many sides, including details on its rich history, magnificent buildings, varied food, and interesting attractions.

Baku's historical attractions, including the Old City (Icherisheher), the Palace of the Shirvanshahs, and the Maiden Tower, transport tourists back in time and illustrate the city's former role as a significant Silk Road commercial center. The mix of contemporary constructions and medieval architecture is fascinating and is guaranteed to astound visitors.

The city's development into a contemporary metropolis is seen in its futuristic skyline, which is emphasized by recognizable buildings like the Heydar Aliyev Center and Flame Towers. Baku's dedication to modernity is also evident in its creative urban design, which includes areas like the Boulevard and the Crystal Hall which are now well-liked meeting spots for both residents and visitors.

Baku's culinary scene is a great joy for food lovers, presenting a variety of cuisines that are indigenous to Azerbaijan and from across the world. Visitors may enjoy a gourmet excursion that exhibits the many tastes and culinary traditions of Azerbaijan, from delectable kebabs and dolma to fragrant teas and pastries.

Baku has a thriving cultural scene in addition to its historical and gastronomic attractions. Numerous museums, galleries, and performance spaces can be found in the city where tourists may learn about Azerbaijani dance, music, and art. The city's dedication to fostering cultural interaction and innovation is best shown through events like the yearly Baku Jazz Festival and the Baku International Film Festival.

Additionally, Baku's natural surroundings provide chances for leisurely outdoor pursuits. Beautiful views and an opportunity to relax can be found along the Caspian Sea shoreline while neighboring Gobustan National Park offers the chance to see old rock sculptures and take in the splendor of Azerbaijan's untamed landscapes.

Baku offers a range of lodging alternatives, including luxury hotels, boutique inns, and affordable lodgings, to suit a variety of tastes and price ranges. A further layer of beauty is added by the friendly hospitality of the residents, who make sure that guests are welcomed and at ease during their stay.

Generally speaking, Baku is a city that skillfully blends its extensive past with modernity, making it a really alluring destination for tourists. Baku has plenty to offer for everyone, whether you want to see historic sites, indulge in delectable food, learn about the local way of life, or just take in the vibrant energy of a busy city. It's a spot that will stay with you and call you to come back so you may find even more of its undiscovered gems.

Printed in Great Britain
by Amazon

25135901R00126